FRESH FUSION

INNOVATIVE RECIPES FOR HEALTHY EATING

NEW/FRESH/FAST/TASTY/HEALTHY

FOR KIDS AND ADULTS TO ENJOY TOGETHER

By Jamie Greenlees

SHRIMP AND MANGO LETTUCE WRAPS

INGREDIENTS:
- 1 LB LARGE SHRIMP, PEELED AND DEVEINED
- 1 RIPE MANGO, DICED
- 1 RED BELL PEPPER, DICED
- 1/4 CUP RED ONION, DICED
- 1 JALAPEÑO PEPPER, SEEDED AND FINELY CHOPPED
- 2 CLOVES GARLIC, MINCED
- 2 TBSP LIME JUICE
- 2 TBSP OLIVE OIL
- SALT AND PEPPER TO TASTE
- BIBB OR BUTTER LETTUCE LEAVES FOR SERVING

INSTRUCTIONS:
1. IN A LARGE BOWL, WHISK TOGETHER THE LIME JUICE, OLIVE OIL, GARLIC, SALT, AND PEPPER.
2. ADD THE SHRIMP TO THE BOWL AND TOSS TO COAT IN THE MARINADE. LET SIT FOR 10-15 MINUTES.
3. HEAT A LARGE SKILLET OVER MEDIUM-HIGH HEAT. ADD THE MARINATED SHRIMP TO THE SKILLET AND COOK FOR 2-3 MINUTES ON EACH SIDE UNTIL PINK AND COOKED THROUGH.
4. WHILE THE SHRIMP COOKS, ASSEMBLE THE LETTUCE WRAPS. TAKE A LETTUCE LEAF AND ADD A FEW PIECES OF DICED MANGO, RED BELL PEPPER, RED ONION, AND JALAPEÑO PEPPER.
5. ONCE THE SHRIMP IS COOKED, ADD A FEW SHRIMP TO EACH LETTUCE WRAP.
6. GARNISH WITH ADDITIONAL LIME JUICE AND CHOPPED CILANTRO, IF DESIRED.
7. SERVE IMMEDIATELY AND ENJOY!

THESE SHRIMP AND MANGO LETTUCE WRAPS ARE A REFRESHING AND HEALTHY LUNCH OPTION THAT IS BOTH FLAVOURFUL AND SATISFYING. THE COMBINATION OF SWEET MANGO AND SPICY JALAPEÑO ADDS A UNIQUE TWIST TO A CLASSIC LETTUCE WRAP.

QUINOA STUFFED BELL PEPPERS

INGREDIENTS:
- 4 BELL PEPPERS, ANY COLOUR
- 1 CUP COOKED QUINOA
- 1 CAN BLACK BEANS, DRAINED AND RINSED
- 1/2 CUP CORN KERNELS
- 1/2 CUP DICED TOMATOES
- 1/4 CUP DICED RED ONION
- 2 CLOVES GARLIC, MINCED
- 1 TSP CUMIN
- 1/2 TSP SMOKED PAPRIKA
- SALT AND PEPPER TO TASTE
- 1/4 CUP SHREDDED CHEDDAR CHEESE (OPTIONAL)

INSTRUCTIONS:
1. PREHEAT THE OVEN TO 375°F.
2. CUT OFF THE TOPS OF THE BELL PEPPERS AND REMOVE THE SEEDS AND MEMBRANES.
3. IN A LARGE BOWL, COMBINE THE COOKED QUINOA, BLACK BEANS, CORN, TOMATOES, RED ONION, GARLIC, CUMIN, SMOKED PAPRIKA, SALT, AND PEPPER.
4. STUFF THE MIXTURE INTO THE BELL PEPPERS AND PLACE THEM UPRIGHT IN A BAKING DISH.
5. IF USING CHEESE, SPRINKLE THE SHREDDED CHEDDAR OVER THE TOPS OF THE STUFFED BELL PEPPERS.
6. COVER THE BAKING DISH WITH FOIL AND BAKE FOR 25-30 MINUTES.
7. REMOVE THE FOIL AND BAKE FOR AN ADDITIONAL 5-10 MINUTES OR UNTIL THE CHEESE IS MELTED AND BUBBLY (IF USING).
8. SERVE THE STUFFED BELL PEPPERS HOT AND ENJOY!

THESE QUINOA STUFFED BELL PEPPERS ARE A HEALTHY AND SATISFYING LUNCH OPTION THAT IS PACKED WITH PROTEIN, FIBRE, AND NUTRIENTS. THEY CAN BE CUSTOMIZED WITH DIFFERENT VEGETABLES, SPICES, AND CHEESE, MAKING THEM A VERSATILE AND DELICIOUS DISH FOR ANY DAY OF THE WEEK.

MEDITERRANEAN CHICKPEA SALAD

INGREDIENTS:
- 1 CAN CHICKPEAS, DRAINED AND RINSED
- 1/2 CUP DICED CUCUMBER
- 1/2 CUP DICED CHERRY TOMATOES
- 1/4 CUP DICED RED ONION
- 1/4 CUP CRUMBLED FETA CHEESE
- 2 TBSP CHOPPED FRESH PARSLEY
- 2 TBSP OLIVE OIL
- 1 TBSP LEMON JUICE
- 1 CLOVE GARLIC, MINCED
- SALT AND PEPPER TO TASTE
- WHOLE GRAIN PITA BREAD OR LETTUCE LEAVES FOR SERVING

INSTRUCTIONS:
1. IN A LARGE BOWL, COMBINE THE CHICKPEAS, CUCUMBER, CHERRY TOMATOES, RED ONION, FETA CHEESE, AND PARSLEY.
2. IN A SMALL BOWL, WHISK TOGETHER THE OLIVE OIL, LEMON JUICE, GARLIC, SALT, AND PEPPER.
3. POUR THE DRESSING OVER THE CHICKPEA MIXTURE AND TOSS TO COAT.
4. SERVE THE CHICKPEA SALAD IN A PITA BREAD OR WRAPPED IN LETTUCE LEAVES.
5. ENJOY!

THIS MEDITERRANEAN CHICKPEA SALAD IS A FLAVOURFUL AND HEALTHY LUNCH OPTION THAT IS PACKED WITH PLANT-BASED PROTEIN, FIBRE, AND NUTRIENTS. THE COMBINATION OF FRESH VEGETABLES, TANGY FETA CHEESE, AND ZESTY LEMON DRESSING CREATES A DELICIOUS AND SATISFYING SALAD THAT CAN BE EASILY CUSTOMIZED TO SUIT YOUR TASTES.

SPICY TUNA AND AVOCADO LETTUCE WRAPS

INGREDIENTS:
- 1 CAN OF TUNA, DRAINED
- 1 RIPE AVOCADO, DICED
- 1/4 CUP RED ONION, DICED
- 1 JALAPEÑO PEPPER, SEEDED AND FINELY CHOPPED
- 2 TBSP LIME JUICE
- 1 TBSP HOT SAUCE (SUCH AS TABASCO)
- SALT AND PEPPER TO TASTE
- DASH OR BUTTER LETTUCE LEAVES FOR SERVING

INSTRUCTIONS:
1. IN A MEDIUM BOWL, COMBINE THE TUNA, DICED AVOCADO, RED ONION, JALAPEÑO PEPPER, LIME JUICE, HOT SAUCE, SALT, AND PEPPER.
2. USE A FORK TO MASH THE MIXTURE TOGETHER, BREAKING UP ANY LARGE CHUNKS OF TUNA.
3. ARRANGE THE LETTUCE LEAVES ON A SERVING PLATE OR PLATTER.
4. SPOON THE SPICY TUNA MIXTURE INTO EACH LETTUCE LEAF.
5. GARNISH WITH ADDITIONAL LIME JUICE, CHOPPED CILANTRO, AND SLICED JALAPEÑO PEPPERS, IF DESIRED.
6. SERVE IMMEDIATELY AND ENJOY!

THESE SPICY TUNA AND AVOCADO LETTUCE WRAPS ARE A HEALTHY AND FLAVOURFUL LUNCH OPTION THAT IS PACKED WITH PROTEIN, HEALTHY FATS, AND VITAMINS. THE COMBINATION OF SPICY TUNA AND CREAMY AVOCADO CREATES A DELICIOUS AND SATISFYING FILLING THAT PAIRS PERFECTLY WITH CRISP LETTUCE LEAVES. IT'S A QUICK AND EASY RECIPE THAT'S PERFECT FOR BUSY WEEKDAYS OR ANYTIME YOU'RE CRAVING SOMETHING LIGHT AND REFRESHING.

SPICY COCONUT SHRIMP SOUP

INGREDIENTS:
- 1 LB SHRIMP, PEELED AND DEVEINED
- 2 TBSP COCONUT OIL
- 1/2 CUP DICED ONION
- 2 CLOVES GARLIC, MINCED
- 1 TBSP GRATED GINGER
- 1 TBSP RED CURRY PASTE
- 1 CAN COCONUT MILK
- 3 CUPS CHICKEN OR VEGETABLE BROTH
- 1 TBSP FISH SAUCE
- 1 TBSP LIME JUICE
- 1 TBSP BROWN SUGAR
- 1/2 TSP SALT
- 1/4 TSP BLACK PEPPER
- 1/4 CUP CHOPPED FRESH CILANTRO
- 1/4 CUP CHOPPED GREEN ONIONS
- LIME WEDGES FOR SERVING

INSTRUCTIONS:
1. HEAT THE COCONUT OIL IN A LARGE POT OVER MEDIUM HEAT.
2. ADD THE DICED ONION, MINCED GARLIC, AND GRATED GINGER TO THE POT AND SAUTÉ UNTIL THE ONION IS SOFT AND TRANSLUCENT.
3. ADD THE RED CURRY PASTE AND STIR TO COAT THE VEGETABLES.
4. ADD THE SHRIMP TO THE POT AND COOK UNTIL PINK AND COOKED THROUGH, ABOUT 3-4 MINUTES.
5. POUR IN THE COCONUT MILK AND CHICKEN OR VEGETABLE BROTH, STIRRING TO COMBINE.
6. ADD THE FISH SAUCE, LIME JUICE, BROWN SUGAR, SALT, AND BLACK PEPPER TO THE POT AND STIR TO COMBINE.
7. BRING THE SOUP TO A SIMMER AND COOK FOR 10-15 MINUTES, STIRRING OCCASIONALLY.
8. REMOVE THE POT FROM HEAT AND STIR IN THE CHOPPED CILANTRO AND GREEN ONIONS.
9. SERVE THE SPICY COCONUT SHRIMP SOUP HOT, GARNISHED WITH LIME WEDGES AND ADDITIONAL CILANTRO, IF DESIRED.

THIS SPICY COCONUT SHRIMP SOUP IS A DELICIOUS AND SATISFYING LUNCH OPTION THAT IS PACKED WITH FLAVOUR AND NUTRIENTS. THE COMBINATION OF CREAMY COCONUT MILK, SPICY RED CURRY PASTE, AND TENDER SHRIMP CREATES A RICH AND SATISFYING SOUP THAT'S PERFECT FOR A COLD OR RAINY DAY. IT'S A QUICK AND EASY RECIPE THAT CAN BE CUSTOMIZED WITH DIFFERENT VEGETABLES, SPICES, AND PROTEINS, MAKING IT A VERSATILE AND DELICIOUS DISH FOR ANY DAY OF THE WEEK.

CHICKPEA AND AVOCADO SALAD WITH LEMON DRESSING

INGREDIENTS:
- 1 CAN CHICKPEAS, DRAINED AND RINSED
- 1 RIPE AVOCADO, DICED
- 1 SMALL CUCUMBER, DICED
- 1 SMALL RED ONION, DICED
- 1/4 CUP CHOPPED FRESH PARSLEY
- 1/4 CUP CHOPPED FRESH MINT
- 1/4 CUP CRUMBLED FETA CHEESE (OPTIONAL)
- 1 TBSP OLIVE OIL
- 2 TBSP LEMON JUICE
- SALT AND PEPPER TO TASTE

INSTRUCTIONS:
1. IN A MEDIUM BOWL, COMBINE THE CHICKPEAS, DICED AVOCADO, DICED CUCUMBER, DICED RED ONION, CHOPPED PARSLEY, AND CHOPPED MINT.
2. IF DESIRED, ADD THE CRUMBLED FETA CHEESE TO THE BOWL.
3. IN A SMALL BOWL, WHISK TOGETHER THE OLIVE OIL AND LEMON JUICE TO MAKE THE DRESSING.
4. POUR THE DRESSING OVER THE CHICKPEA AND AVOCADO MIXTURE AND TOSS TO COAT.
5. SEASON THE SALAD WITH SALT AND PEPPER TO TASTE.
6. SERVE THE CHICKPEA AND AVOCADO SALAD IMMEDIATELY, GARNISHED WITH ADDITIONAL HERBS, IF DESIRED.

THIS CHICKPEA AND AVOCADO SALAD IS A HEALTHY AND DELICIOUS LUNCH DISH THAT'S PERFECT FOR A QUICK AND EASY MEAL. IT'S PACKED WITH FIBRE, HEALTHY FATS, AND PROTEIN, AND THE COMBINATION OF FRESH HERBS AND TANGY LEMON DRESSING CREATES A FLAVOURFUL AND REFRESHING SALAD THAT'S SURE TO SATISFY. IT CAN BE CUSTOMIZED WITH DIFFERENT VEGETABLES, HERBS, AND DRESSINGS TO SUIT YOUR TASTES, MAKING IT A VERSATILE AND DELICIOUS DISH FOR ANY DAY OF THE WEEK.

SOBA NOODLE SALAD WITH EDAMAME AND PEANUT DRESSING

INGREDIENTS:

- 4 OZ SOBA NOODLES
- 1 CUP SHELLED EDAMAME
- 1 CUP SHREDDED CARROTS
- 1/2 CUP CHOPPED SCALLIONS
- 1/4 CUP CHOPPED CILANTRO
- 1/4 CUP CHOPPED ROASTED PEANUTS
- 2 TBSP RICE VINEGAR
- 2 TBSP SOY SAUCE
- 1 TBSP HONEY
- 1 TBSP CREAMY PEANUT BUTTER
- 1 CLOVE GARLIC, MINCED
- 1 TSP GRATED FRESH GINGER
- 1 TBSP SESAME OIL
- SALT AND PEPPER TO TASTE

INSTRUCTIONS:

1. COOK THE SOBA NOODLES ACCORDING TO PACKAGE DIRECTIONS UNTIL AL DENTE. DRAIN AND RINSE THE NOODLES UNDER COLD WATER TO STOP THE COOKING PROCESS.
2. IN A LARGE BOWL, COMBINE THE COOKED SOBA NOODLES, SHELLED EDAMAME, SHREDDED CARROTS, CHOPPED SCALLIONS, CHOPPED CILANTRO, AND CHOPPED ROASTED PEANUTS.
3. IN A SEPARATE SMALL BOWL, WHISK TOGETHER THE RICE VINEGAR, SOY SAUCE, HONEY, PEANUT BUTTER, MINCED GARLIC, GRATED GINGER, AND SESAME OIL TO MAKE THE DRESSING.
4. POUR THE DRESSING OVER THE SOBA NOODLE MIXTURE AND TOSS TO COAT EVENLY.
5. SEASON THE SALAD WITH SALT AND PEPPER TO TASTE.
6. SERVE THE SOBA NOODLE SALAD IMMEDIATELY, GARNISHED WITH ADDITIONAL CHOPPED PEANUTS AND CILANTRO, IF DESIRED.

THIS SOBA NOODLE SALAD WITH EDAMAME AND PEANUT DRESSING IS A UNIQUE AND HEALTHY LUNCH DISH THAT'S PACKED WITH PROTEIN, FIBRE, AND FLAVOUR. THE COMBINATION OF TENDER SOBA NOODLES, CRUNCHY EDAMAME, AND FLAVOURFUL VEGETABLES, TOSSED IN A CREAMY AND SAVOURY PEANUT DRESSING, CREATES A SATISFYING AND DELICIOUS SALAD THAT'S PERFECT FOR A QUICK AND EASY MEAL. IT CAN BE CUSTOMIZED WITH DIFFERENT VEGETABLES, NUTS, AND DRESSINGS TO SUIT YOUR TASTES, MAKING IT A VERSATILE AND DELICIOUS DISH FOR ANY DAY OF THE WEEK.

MEDITERRANEAN QUINOA SALAD WITH FETA AND LEMON DRESSING

INGREDIENTS:
- 1 CUP QUINOA, RINSED AND DRAINED
- 2 CUPS WATER OR VEGETABLE BROTH
- 1 RED BELL PEPPER, DICED
- 1 YELLOW BELL PEPPER, DICED
- 1 SMALL RED ONION, DICED
- 1 CUP CHERRY TOMATOES, HALVED
- 1 CUP CRUMBLED FETA CHEESE
- 1/4 CUP CHOPPED FRESH PARSLEY
- 1/4 CUP CHOPPED FRESH MINT
- 1/4 CUP PITTED KALAMATA OLIVES, HALVED
- 2 TBSP OLIVE OIL
- 2 TBSP LEMON JUICE
- 1 CLOVE GARLIC, MINCED
- SALT AND PEPPER TO TASTE

INSTRUCTIONS:

1. IN A MEDIUM SAUCEPAN, COMBINE THE QUINOA AND WATER OR VEGETABLE BROTH. BRING TO A BOIL, THEN REDUCE THE HEAT TO LOW AND SIMMER FOR 15-20 MINUTES, OR UNTIL THE QUINOA IS TENDER AND THE LIQUID IS ABSORBED.

2. IN A LARGE BOWL, COMBINE THE COOKED QUINOA, DICED RED AND YELLOW BELL PEPPERS, DICED RED ONION, HALVED CHERRY TOMATOES, CRUMBLED FETA CHEESE, CHOPPED PARSLEY AND MINT, AND HALVED KALAMATA OLIVES.

3. IN A SMALL BOWL, WHISK TOGETHER THE OLIVE OIL, LEMON JUICE, MINCED GARLIC, SALT, AND PEPPER TO MAKE THE DRESSING.

4. POUR THE DRESSING OVER THE QUINOA SALAD AND TOSS TO COAT EVENLY.

5. SERVE THE MEDITERRANEAN QUINOA SALAD IMMEDIATELY, GARNISHED WITH ADDITIONAL HERBS AND OLIVES, IF DESIRED.

THIS MEDITERRANEAN QUINOA SALAD WITH FETA AND LEMON DRESSING IS A UNIQUE AND HEALTHY LUNCH DISH THAT'S PACKED WITH PROTEIN, FIBRE, AND FLAVOUR. THE COMBINATION OF FLUFFY QUINOA, CRUNCHY VEGETABLES, TANGY FETA CHEESE, AND BRINY OLIVES, ALL DRESSED IN A ZESTY AND REFRESHING LEMON DRESSING, CREATES A SATISFYING AND DELICIOUS SALAD THAT'S PERFECT FOR A QUICK AND EASY MEAL. IT CAN BE CUSTOMIZED WITH DIFFERENT VEGETABLES, HERBS, AND DRESSINGS TO SUIT YOUR TASTES, MAKING IT A VERSATILE AND DELICIOUS DISH FOR ANY DAY OF THE WEEK.

CHARRED CAULIFLOWER AND CHICKPEA SALAD WITH ZA'ATAR DRESSING

INGREDIENTS:
- 1 HEAD OF CAULIFLOWER, CUT INTO FLORETS
- 1 CAN OF CHICKPEAS, DRAINED AND RINSED
- 1/4 CUP CHOPPED FRESH PARSLEY
- 1/4 CUP CHOPPED FRESH CILANTRO
- 1/4 CUP CHOPPED DRIED APRICOTS
- 1/4 CUP CHOPPED TOASTED PISTACHIOS
- 1/4 CUP CRUMBLED FETA CHEESE
- 2 TBSP OLIVE OIL
- 2 TBSP LEMON JUICE
- 1 TBSP ZA'ATAR SPICE BLEND
- 1 CLOVE GARLIC, MINCED
- SALT AND PEPPER TO TASTE

INSTRUCTIONS:
1. PREHEAT A GRILL OR GRILL PAN TO MEDIUM-HIGH HEAT.
2. IN A LARGE BOWL, TOSS THE CAULIFLOWER FLORETS WITH 1 TABLESPOON OF OLIVE OIL AND SEASON WITH SALT AND PEPPER.
3. PLACE THE CAULIFLOWER FLORETS ON THE GRILL OR GRILL PAN AND COOK FOR 8-10 MINUTES, OR UNTIL CHARRED AND TENDER. REMOVE FROM HEAT AND SET ASIDE.
4. IN A LARGE BOWL, COMBINE THE COOKED CHICKPEAS, CHOPPED PARSLEY AND CILANTRO, CHOPPED DRIED APRICOTS, CHOPPED TOASTED PISTACHIOS, AND CRUMBLED FETA CHEESE.
5. IN A SMALL BOWL, WHISK TOGETHER THE REMAINING 1 TABLESPOON OF OLIVE OIL, LEMON JUICE, ZA'ATAR SPICE BLEND, MINCED GARLIC, SALT, AND PEPPER TO MAKE THE DRESSING.
6. POUR THE DRESSING OVER THE CHICKPEA SALAD AND TOSS TO COAT EVENLY.
7. ADD THE CHARRED CAULIFLOWER FLORETS TO THE SALAD AND GENTLY TOSS TO COMBINE.
8. SERVE THE CHARRED CAULIFLOWER AND CHICKPEA SALAD IMMEDIATELY, GARNISHED WITH ADDITIONAL CHOPPED HERBS AND PISTACHIOS, IF DESIRED.

THIS CHARRED CAULIFLOWER AND CHICKPEA SALAD WITH ZA'ATAR DRESSING IS A UNIQUE AND HEALTHY LUNCH DISH THAT'S PACKED WITH FLAVOUR AND NUTRITION. THE COMBINATION OF SMOKY AND TENDER CAULIFLOWER, HEARTY AND PROTEIN-RICH CHICKPEAS, AND A MEDLEY OF SWEET AND SAVOURY INGREDIENTS, ALL DRESSED IN A TANGY AND AROMATIC ZA'ATAR DRESSING, CREATES A SATISFYING AND DELICIOUS SALAD THAT'S PERFECT FOR A QUICK AND EASY MEAL. IT CAN BE CUSTOMIZED WITH DIFFERENT VEGETABLES, NUTS, AND DRESSINGS TO SUIT YOUR TASTES, MAKING IT A VERSATILE AND DELICIOUS DISH FOR ANY DAY OF THE WEEK.

SPICY TOFU AND MUSHROOM LETTUCE WRAPS

INGREDIENTS:
- 1 BLOCK OF FIRM TOFU, DRAINED AND DICED
- 1 CUP SLICED MUSHROOMS
- 1 RED BELL PEPPER, DICED
- 1/2 CUP CHOPPED SCALLIONS
- 1/4 CUP CHOPPED FRESH CILANTRO
- 1/4 CUP CHOPPED FRESH MINT
- 2 TBSP SOY SAUCE
- 2 TBSP RICE VINEGAR
- 1 TBSP CHILI GARLIC SAUCE
- 1 TBSP SESAME OIL
- 1 TBSP HONEY
- 1 HEAD OF BUTTER LETTUCE, LEAVES SEPARATED
- 1/4 CUP CHOPPED PEANUTS (OPTIONAL)

INSTRUCTIONS:
1. IN A LARGE SKILLET, HEAT 1 TABLESPOON OF SESAME OIL OVER MEDIUM-HIGH HEAT.
2. ADD THE DICED TOFU AND SLICED MUSHROOMS AND COOK FOR 5-7 MINUTES, OR UNTIL BROWNED AND CRISPY.
3. ADD THE DICED RED BELL PEPPER AND CHOPPED SCALLIONS AND COOK FOR ANOTHER 3-5 MINUTES, OR UNTIL THE VEGETABLES ARE TENDER.
4. IN A SMALL BOWL, WHISK TOGETHER THE SOY SAUCE, RICE VINEGAR, CHILI GARLIC SAUCE, SESAME OIL, AND HONEY TO MAKE THE SPICY SAUCE.
5. ADD THE SPICY SAUCE TO THE SKILLET AND STIR TO COAT THE TOFU AND VEGETABLES EVENLY. COOK FOR 1-2 MINUTES, OR UNTIL THE SAUCE THICKENS.
6. REMOVE THE SKILLET FROM THE HEAT AND STIR IN THE CHOPPED CILANTRO AND MINT.
7. TO ASSEMBLE THE LETTUCE WRAPS, TAKE A BUTTER LETTUCE LEAF AND SPOON A GENEROUS AMOUNT OF THE TOFU AND MUSHROOM FILLING ONTO IT. SPRINKLE WITH CHOPPED PEANUTS, IF DESIRED.
8. ROLL THE LETTUCE LEAF AROUND THE FILLING AND SERVE THE SPICY TOFU AND MUSHROOM LETTUCE WRAPS IMMEDIATELY.

THESE SPICY TOFU AND MUSHROOM LETTUCE WRAPS ARE A UNIQUE AND HEALTHY LUNCH DISH THAT'S PACKED WITH PROTEIN, FIBRE, AND FLAVOUR. THE COMBINATION OF CRISPY AND SAVOURY TOFU, MEATY AND EARTHY MUSHROOMS, AND A MEDLEY OF BOLD AND AROMATIC SPICES, ALL WRAPPED IN CRISP AND REFRESHING BUTTER LETTUCE LEAVES, CREATES A SATISFYING AND DELICIOUS DISH THAT'S PERFECT FOR A QUICK AND EASY MEAL. IT CAN BE CUSTOMIZED WITH DIFFERENT VEGETABLES, HERBS, AND SAUCES TO SUIT YOUR TASTES, MAKING IT A VERSATILE AND DELICIOUS DISH FOR ANY DAY OF THE WEEK.

FOR THE TURMERIC ROASTED CHICKPEAS:

- 1 CAN OF CHICKPEAS, DRAINED AND RINSED
- 1 TSP GROUND TURMERIC
- 1 TSP GROUND CUMIN
- 1/2 TSP GARLIC POWDER
- 1/2 TSP SEA SALT
- 1 TBSP OLIVE OIL

FOR THE CAULIFLOWER RICE BOWL:

- 1 HEAD OF CAULIFLOWER, CHOPPED INTO FLORETS
- 1 RED BELL PEPPER, DICED
- 1/2 RED ONION, DICED
- 1 AVOCADO, PEELED AND PITTED
- 1/4 CUP PLAIN GREEK YOGURT
- 1 CLOVE GARLIC, MINCED
- JUICE OF 1 LIME
- SALT AND PEPPER TO TASTE
- FRESH CILANTRO FOR GARNISH

INSTRUCTIONS:

1. PREHEAT THE OVEN TO 400°F (200°C).
2. IN A BOWL, COMBINE THE DRAINED CHICKPEAS, TURMERIC, CUMIN, GARLIC POWDER, SEA SALT, AND OLIVE OIL. MIX WELL UNTIL THE CHICKPEAS ARE COATED.
3. SPREAD THE CHICKPEAS OUT ON A BAKING SHEET AND ROAST FOR 20-25 MINUTES OR UNTIL CRISPY.
4. WHILE THE CHICKPEAS ARE ROASTING, PULSE THE CAULIFLOWER FLORETS IN A FOOD PROCESSOR UNTIL THEY RESEMBLE RICE.
5. IN A PAN, SAUTÉ THE CAULIFLOWER RICE, DICED RED BELL PEPPER, AND DICED RED ONION OVER MEDIUM-HIGH HEAT FOR 5-7 MINUTES, OR UNTIL THE VEGETABLES ARE TENDER.
6. TO MAKE THE AVOCADO SAUCE, BLEND THE PEELED AND PITTED AVOCADO, PLAIN GREEK YOGURT, MINCED GARLIC, LIME JUICE, SALT, AND PEPPER IN A FOOD PROCESSOR UNTIL SMOOTH.
7. TO ASSEMBLE THE CAULIFLOWER RICE BOWL, DIVIDE THE CAULIFLOWER RICE MIXTURE BETWEEN TWO BOWLS. TOP WITH THE ROASTED TURMERIC CHICKPEAS AND DRIZZLE WITH THE AVOCADO SAUCE. GARNISH WITH FRESH CILANTRO AND SERVE IMMEDIATELY.

THIS CAULIFLOWER RICE BOWL WITH TURMERIC ROASTED CHICKPEAS AND AVOCADO SAUCE IS A UNIQUE AND HEALTHY LUNCH DISH THAT'S PACKED WITH PLANT-BASED PROTEIN, FIBRE, AND ANTI-INFLAMMATORY PROPERTIES. THE COMBINATION OF FRAGRANT AND FLAVOURFUL SPICES, TENDER AND NUTRIENT-DENSE CAULIFLOWER RICE, CRISPY AND SATISFYING ROASTED CHICKPEAS, AND CREAMY AND ZESTY AVOCADO SAUCE CREATES A DELICIOUS AND NUTRITIOUS MEAL THAT'S PERFECT FOR A QUICK AND EASY LUNCH. IT CAN BE CUSTOMIZED WITH DIFFERENT VEGETABLES, HERBS, AND SAUCES TO SUIT YOUR TASTES, MAKING IT A VERSATILE AND SATISFYING DISH FOR ANY DAY OF THE WEEK.

SPICY LENTIL AND VEGETABLE STIR-FRY WITH PEANUT SAUCE (PART 1)

INGREDIENTS:

FOR THE STIR-FRY:

- 1 CUP DRIED GREEN OR BROWN LENTILS, RINSED AND DRAINED
- 1 LARGE CARROT, PEELED AND SLICED INTO THIN ROUNDS
- 1 RED BELL PEPPER, SLICED INTO THIN STRIPS
- 1 SMALL RED ONION, THINLY SLICED
- 2 CLOVES GARLIC, MINCED
- 1 TBSP GRATED FRESH GINGER
- 1 TBSP COCONUT OIL
- 1 TSP GROUND CUMIN
- 1 TSP SMOKED PAPRIKA
- 1/2 TSP CAYENNE PEPPER
- SALT AND PEPPER TO TASTE
- FRESH CILANTRO FOR GARNISH

FOR THE PEANUT SAUCE:

- 1/4 CUP CREAMY PEANUT BUTTER
- 2 TBSP LOW-SODIUM SOY SAUCE
- 1 TBSP HONEY OR MAPLE SYRUP
- 1 TBSP RICE VINEGAR
- 1 CLOVE GARLIC, MINCED
- 1 TSP GRATED FRESH GINGER
- 1/4 TSP RED PEPPER FLAKES (OPTIONAL)
- WATER AS NEEDED TO THIN THE SAUCE

PART 2

INSTRUCTIONS:

1. IN A MEDIUM SAUCEPAN, BRING THE LENTILS AND 2 CUPS OF WATER TO A BOIL. REDUCE THE HEAT TO LOW, COVER, AND SIMMER FOR 20-25 MINUTES OR UNTIL THE LENTILS ARE TENDER. DRAIN ANY EXCESS WATER AND SET ASIDE.

2. IN A LARGE SKILLET OR WOK, HEAT THE COCONUT OIL OVER MEDIUM-HIGH HEAT. ADD THE SLICED CARROT, RED BELL PEPPER, AND RED ONION AND STIR-FRY FOR 5-7 MINUTES OR UNTIL THE VEGETABLES ARE TENDER.

3. ADD THE MINCED GARLIC, GRATED GINGER, GROUND CUMIN, SMOKED PAPRIKA, CAYENNE PEPPER, SALT, AND PEPPER TO THE SKILLET OR WOK AND STIR-FRY FOR ANOTHER MINUTE OR UNTIL FRAGRANT.

4. ADD THE COOKED LENTILS TO THE SKILLET OR WOK AND STIR-FRY FOR 2-3 MINUTES OR UNTIL HEATED THROUGH.

5. TO MAKE THE PEANUT SAUCE, WHISK TOGETHER THE PEANUT BUTTER, LOW-SODIUM SOY SAUCE, HONEY OR MAPLE SYRUP, RICE VINEGAR, MINCED GARLIC, GRATED GINGER, AND RED PEPPER FLAKES (IF USING) IN A SMALL BOWL. ADD WATER AS NEEDED TO THIN THE SAUCE TO YOUR DESIRED CONSISTENCY.

6. SERVE THE SPICY LENTIL AND VEGETABLE STIR-FRY IN BOWLS, DRIZZLED WITH THE PEANUT SAUCE AND GARNISHED WITH FRESH CILANTRO.

THIS SPICY LENTIL AND VEGETABLE STIR-FRY WITH PEANUT SAUCE IS A FLAVOURFUL AND NUTRITIOUS LUNCH DISH THAT'S HIGH IN PROTEIN, FIBRE, AND HEALTHY FATS. THE COMBINATION OF TENDER AND HEARTY LENTILS, CRUNCHY AND COLOURFUL VEGETABLES, AND SPICY AND SAVOURY SEASONINGS CREATES A SATISFYING AND DELICIOUS MEAL THAT'S PERFECT FOR A QUICK AND EASY LUNCH. THE CREAMY AND NUTTY PEANUT SAUCE ADDS A RICH AND COMPLEX FLAVOUR THAT BALANCES THE HEAT AND SWEETNESS OF THE STIR-FRY, MAKING IT A WELL-ROUNDED AND SATISFYING DISH FOR ANY DAY OF THE WEEK. IT CAN BE CUSTOMIZED WITH DIFFERENT VEGETABLES, HERBS, AND SAUCES TO SUIT YOUR TASTES, MAKING IT A VERSATILE AND TASTY RECIPE TO TRY.

SUPERFOOD QUINOA BOWL WITH AVOCADO AND KALE

INGREDIENTS:

- 1 CUP QUINOA, RINSED AND DRAINED
- 2 CUPS WATER OR LOW-SODIUM VEGETABLE BROTH
- 1 LARGE AVOCADO, PITTED AND SLICED
- 1 BUNCH KALE, STEMS REMOVED AND LEAVES CHOPPED
- 1 SMALL RED ONION, THINLY SLICED
- 1 SMALL CUCUMBER, SLICED
- 1 SMALL CARROT, SHREDDED
- 1 SMALL BEET, SHREDDED
- 1/4 CUP RAW PUMPKIN SEEDS
- 2 TBSP EXTRA-VIRGIN OLIVE OIL
- 1 TBSP LEMON JUICE
- 1 CLOVE GARLIC, MINCED
- SALT AND PEPPER TO TASTE

INSTRUCTIONS:

1. IN A MEDIUM SAUCEPAN, COMBINE THE QUINOA AND WATER OR BROTH AND BRING TO A BOIL OVER HIGH HEAT. REDUCE THE HEAT TO LOW, COVER, AND SIMMER FOR 15-20 MINUTES OR UNTIL THE QUINOA IS TENDER AND THE LIQUID HAS BEEN ABSORBED. REMOVE FROM HEAT AND FLUFF WITH A FORK.

2. IN A LARGE SKILLET OR WOK, HEAT THE OLIVE OIL OVER MEDIUM-HIGH HEAT. ADD THE CHOPPED KALE AND SAUTÉ FOR 3-4 MINUTES OR UNTIL WILTED AND TENDER. ADD THE MINCED GARLIC AND SAUTÉ FOR ANOTHER MINUTE OR UNTIL FRAGRANT.

3. TO ASSEMBLE THE BOWLS, DIVIDE THE COOKED QUINOA, SAUTÉED KALE, SLICED AVOCADO, SLICED RED ONION, SLICED CUCUMBER, SHREDDED CARROT, AND SHREDDED BEET AMONG 4 BOWLS. SPRINKLE WITH RAW PUMPKIN SEEDS.

4. IN A SMALL BOWL, WHISK TOGETHER THE LEMON JUICE, SALT, AND PEPPER. DRIZZLE OVER EACH BOWL AND SERVE IMMEDIATELY.

THIS SUPERFOOD QUINOA BOWL WITH AVOCADO AND KALE IS PACKED WITH NUTRITIOUS AND DELICIOUS INGREDIENTS THAT ARE LOADED WITH VITAMINS, MINERALS, FIBRE, AND HEALTHY FATS. QUINOA IS A HIGH-PROTEIN GRAIN THAT'S ALSO GLUTEN-FREE AND EASY TO DIGEST, MAKING IT A GREAT ALTERNATIVE TO OTHER GRAINS. KALE IS A LEAFY GREEN THAT'S RICH IN VITAMINS A, C, AND K, AS WELL AS CALCIUM AND IRON. AVOCADO IS A HEART-HEALTHY FRUIT THAT'S HIGH IN MONOUNSATURATED FATS AND FIBRE, AND ALSO CONTAINS VITAMINS C AND K. THE OTHER VEGGIES, SUCH AS RED ONION, CUCUMBER, CARROT, AND BEET, ARE ALSO RICH IN VITAMINS AND MINERALS. RAW PUMPKIN SEEDS ADD A CRUNCHY TEXTURE AND ARE PACKED WITH HEALTHY FATS, PROTEIN, AND FIBRE. THIS BOWL IS NOT ONLY NUTRITIOUS, BUT ALSO VERY SATISFYING AND FLAVOURFUL, MAKING IT A GREAT LUNCH OPTION FOR ANY DAY OF THE WEEK.

SPICED LENTIL AND SWEET POTATO SALAD

INGREDIENTS:
- 1 CUP BROWN LENTILS, RINSED AND DRAINED
- 2 MEDIUM SWEET POTATOES, PEELED AND CUT INTO 1-INCH CUBES
- 1 RED BELL PEPPER, CHOPPED
- 1/2 RED ONION, CHOPPED
- 1/4 CUP CHOPPED FRESH PARSLEY
- 1/4 CUP CHOPPED FRESH CILANTRO
- 1/4 CUP EXTRA-VIRGIN OLIVE OIL
- 2 TBSP APPLE CIDER VINEGAR
- 1 TSP GROUND CUMIN
- 1 TSP GROUND CORIANDER
- 1/2 TSP SMOKED PAPRIKA
- 1/4 TSP CAYENNE PEPPER
- SALT AND BLACK PEPPER TO TASTE

INSTRUCTIONS:
1. IN A MEDIUM SAUCEPAN, COMBINE THE LENTILS AND 3 CUPS OF WATER. BRING TO A BOIL OVER HIGH HEAT, THEN REDUCE THE HEAT TO LOW AND SIMMER FOR 20-25 MINUTES OR UNTIL THE LENTILS ARE TENDER BUT STILL FIRM. DRAIN ANY EXCESS LIQUID AND SET ASIDE.
2. PREHEAT THE OVEN TO 400°F (200°C). PLACE THE CUBED SWEET POTATOES ON A BAKING SHEET AND TOSS WITH 1 TBSP OF OLIVE OIL. ROAST FOR 20-25 MINUTES OR UNTIL TENDER AND LIGHTLY BROWNED.
3. IN A SMALL BOWL, WHISK TOGETHER THE REMAINING OLIVE OIL, APPLE CIDER VINEGAR, CUMIN, CORIANDER, SMOKED PAPRIKA, CAYENNE PEPPER, SALT, AND BLACK PEPPER.
4. IN A LARGE BOWL, COMBINE THE COOKED LENTILS, ROASTED SWEET POTATOES, CHOPPED RED BELL PEPPER, CHOPPED RED ONION, PARSLEY, CILANTRO, AND THE DRESSING. TOSS TO COAT EVENLY.
5. SERVE THE SPICED LENTIL AND SWEET POTATO SALAD WARM OR AT ROOM TEMPERATURE.

THIS LENTIL AND SWEET POTATO SALAD IS A HEARTY AND FLAVOURFUL DISH THAT'S ALSO RICH IN FIBRE, PROTEIN, VITAMINS, AND MINERALS. LENTILS ARE A GREAT SOURCE OF PLANT-BASED PROTEIN AND FIBRE, AND ARE ALSO RICH IN IRON AND FOLATE. SWEET POTATOES ARE A NUTRIENT-DENSE ROOT VEGETABLE THAT'S HIGH IN FIBRE, VITAMIN A, VITAMIN C, AND POTASSIUM. THE SPICES IN THE DRESSING ADD A WARM AND SMOKY FLAVOUR TO THE DISH, WHILE THE FRESH HERBS ADD A BRIGHT AND FRESH TOUCH. THIS SALAD CAN BE ENJOYED AS A MAIN DISH OR AS A SIDE DISH, AND CAN BE SERVED WARM OR AT ROOM TEMPERATURE.

QUINOA AND GRILLED VEGETABLE SALAD

INGREDIENTS:
- 1 CUP UNCOOKED QUINOA
- 1 RED BELL PEPPER, SEEDED AND SLICED
- 1 YELLOW SQUASH, SLICED
- 1 ZUCCHINI, SLICED
- 1 RED ONION, SLICED
- 2 CUPS MIXED GREENS
- 1/4 CUP CHOPPED FRESH BASIL
- 1/4 CUP CHOPPED FRESH PARSLEY
- 1/4 CUP EXTRA-VIRGIN OLIVE OIL
- 2 TBSP BALSAMIC VINEGAR
- 2 TBSP LEMON JUICE
- 2 CLOVES GARLIC, MINCED
- SALT AND BLACK PEPPER TO TASTE

INSTRUCTIONS:
1. RINSE THE QUINOA IN A FINE-MESH STRAINER AND TRANSFER TO A MEDIUM SAUCEPAN. ADD 2 CUPS OF WATER AND A PINCH OF SALT, AND BRING TO A BOIL OVER HIGH HEAT. REDUCE THE HEAT TO LOW, COVER, AND SIMMER FOR 15-20 MINUTES OR UNTIL THE WATER IS ABSORBED AND THE QUINOA IS TENDER. REMOVE FROM HEAT AND LET COOL.
2. PREHEAT A GRILL OR GRILL PAN TO MEDIUM-HIGH HEAT. BRUSH THE SLICED VEGETABLES WITH OLIVE OIL AND SEASON WITH SALT AND BLACK PEPPER. GRILL THE VEGETABLES FOR 4-5 MINUTES PER SIDE OR UNTIL TENDER AND LIGHTLY CHARRED. REMOVE FROM THE GRILL AND LET COOL.
3. IN A SMALL BOWL, WHISK TOGETHER THE OLIVE OIL, BALSAMIC VINEGAR, LEMON JUICE, GARLIC, SALT, AND BLACK PEPPER.
4. IN A LARGE BOWL, COMBINE THE COOKED QUINOA, GRILLED VEGETABLES, MIXED GREENS, CHOPPED BASIL, CHOPPED PARSLEY, AND THE DRESSING. TOSS TO COAT EVENLY.
5. SERVE THE QUINOA AND GRILLED VEGETABLE SALAD AT ROOM TEMPERATURE.

THIS QUINOA AND GRILLED VEGETABLE SALAD IS A DELICIOUS AND NUTRITIOUS DISH THAT'S PACKED WITH FIBRE, VITAMINS, AND MINERALS. QUINOA IS A PROTEIN-RICH GRAIN THAT'S ALSO HIGH IN FIBRE, IRON, AND MAGNESIUM. GRILLED VEGETABLES ARE A FLAVOURFUL AND COLOURFUL ADDITION TO THE DISH, AND PROVIDE A WIDE RANGE OF VITAMINS AND ANTIOXIDANTS. THE DRESSING IS MADE WITH HEALTHY FATS AND ADDS A TANGY AND SAVOURY FLAVOUR TO THE SALAD. THIS DISH CAN BE ENJOYED AS A MAIN DISH OR AS A SIDE DISH, AND IS PERFECT FOR A HEALTHY AND SATISFYING LUNCH.

MEDITERRANEAN CHICKEN WRAP

INGREDIENTS:
- 1 LARGE WHOLE WHEAT TORTILLA
- 4 OZ COOKED CHICKEN BREAST, SHREDDED
- 1/4 CUP HUMMUS
- 1/4 CUP CHOPPED CUCUMBER
- 1/4 CUP CHOPPED CHERRY TOMATOES
- 1/4 CUP CRUMBLED FETA CHEESE
- 1 TBSP CHOPPED FRESH PARSLEY
- 1 TBSP LEMON JUICE
- SALT AND BLACK PEPPER TO TASTE

INSTRUCTIONS:
1. LAY THE WHOLE WHEAT TORTILLA FLAT ON A PLATE.
2. SPREAD THE HUMMUS EVENLY OVER THE TORTILLA, LEAVING A SMALL BORDER AROUND THE EDGES.
3. SPRINKLE THE SHREDDED CHICKEN OVER THE HUMMUS.
4. TOP WITH CHOPPED CUCUMBER, CHERRY TOMATOES, CRUMBLED FETA CHEESE, AND CHOPPED PARSLEY.
5. DRIZZLE THE LEMON JUICE OVER THE FILLING AND SEASON WITH SALT AND BLACK PEPPER.
6. ROLL THE TORTILLA TIGHTLY, TUCKING IN THE SIDES AS YOU GO, TO FORM A WRAP.
7. SLICE THE WRAP IN HALF AND SERVE.

THIS MEDITERRANEAN CHICKEN WRAP IS A DELICIOUS AND HEALTHY LUNCH OPTION THAT'S PACKED WITH FLAVOUR AND NUTRITION. THE WHOLE WHEAT TORTILLA PROVIDES FIBRE AND COMPLEX CARBOHYDRATES, WHILE THE CHICKEN ADDS LEAN PROTEIN. THE HUMMUS IS A GOOD SOURCE OF HEALTHY FATS AND ALSO ADDS A CREAMY AND SAVOURY FLAVOUR TO THE WRAP. THE CHOPPED VEGETABLES PROVIDE VITAMINS AND ANTIOXIDANTS, AND THE FETA CHEESE ADDS A TANGY AND SALTY TASTE. THE LEMON JUICE AND FRESH PARSLEY ADD BRIGHTNESS AND FRESHNESS TO THE DISH. THIS WRAP CAN BE EASILY CUSTOMIZED WITH YOUR FAVOURITE VEGETABLES OR PROTEIN, AND IS PERFECT FOR A QUICK AND SATISFYING LUNCH

LEMON HERB SALMON WITH ASPARAGUS AND QUINOA

INGREDIENTS:
- 1 LB SALMON FILLET
- 1 LB ASPARAGUS, TRIMMED
- 1 CUP UNCOOKED QUINOA
- 1/4 CUP FRESH LEMON JUICE
- 2 TBSP CHOPPED FRESH PARSLEY
- 2 TBSP CHOPPED FRESH DILL
- 1 TBSP CHOPPED FRESH THYME
- 2 CLOVES GARLIC, MINCED
- 2 TBSP EXTRA-VIRGIN OLIVE OIL
- SALT AND BLACK PEPPER TO TASTE

INSTRUCTIONS:
1. PREHEAT THE OVEN TO 400°F.
2. RINSE THE QUINOA IN A FINE-MESH STRAINER AND TRANSFER TO A MEDIUM SAUCEPAN. ADD 2 CUPS OF WATER AND A PINCH OF SALT, AND BRING TO A BOIL OVER HIGH HEAT. REDUCE THE HEAT TO LOW, COVER, AND SIMMER FOR 15-20 MINUTES OR UNTIL THE WATER IS ABSORBED AND THE QUINOA IS TENDER. REMOVE FROM HEAT AND LET COOL.
3. IN A SMALL BOWL, WHISK TOGETHER THE LEMON JUICE, CHOPPED PARSLEY, CHOPPED DILL, CHOPPED THYME, MINCED GARLIC, 1 TBSP OLIVE OIL, SALT, AND BLACK PEPPER.
4. PLACE THE SALMON FILLET ON A BAKING SHEET LINED WITH PARCHMENT PAPER. BRUSH THE SALMON WITH THE LEMON HERB MIXTURE.
5. TOSS THE TRIMMED ASPARAGUS WITH 1 TBSP OLIVE OIL, SALT, AND BLACK PEPPER. PLACE THE ASPARAGUS ON THE BAKING SHEET NEXT TO THE SALMON.
6. ROAST THE SALMON AND ASPARAGUS IN THE OVEN FOR 12-15 MINUTES OR UNTIL THE SALMON IS COOKED THROUGH AND THE ASPARAGUS IS TENDER.
7. SERVE THE SALMON AND ASPARAGUS WITH THE COOKED QUINOA.

THIS LEMON HERB SALMON WITH ASPARAGUS AND QUINOA IS A HEALTHY AND DELICIOUS LUNCH DISH THAT'S RICH IN PROTEIN, HEALTHY FATS, AND COMPLEX CARBOHYDRATES. THE SALMON IS A GOOD SOURCE OF OMEGA-3 FATTY ACIDS AND PROVIDES A MILD AND BUTTERY FLAVOUR THAT'S COMPLEMENTED BY THE LEMON HERB SAUCE. THE ASPARAGUS IS A NUTRITIOUS AND FLAVOURFUL VEGETABLE THAT'S PACKED WITH VITAMINS AND MINERALS. THE QUINOA IS A PROTEIN-RICH GRAIN THAT'S ALSO HIGH IN FIBRE AND MINERALS. THE HERBS AND GARLIC ADD A BRIGHT AND FRAGRANT TASTE TO THE DISH. THIS LUNCH DISH IS PERFECT FOR A QUICK AND EASY MEAL THAT'S BOTH SATISFYING AND NUTRITIOUS.

GRILLED PEACH AND CHICKEN SALAD WITH HONEY MUSTARD DRESSING

INGREDIENTS:
- 2 PEACHES, SLICED IN HALF AND PITTED
- 2 BONELESS, SKINLESS CHICKEN BREASTS
- 6 CUPS MIXED GREENS
- 1/2 CUP CHERRY TOMATOES, HALVED
- 1/4 CUP CRUMBLED GOAT CHEESE
- 1/4 CUP SLIVERED ALMONDS
- 1/4 CUP CHOPPED FRESH BASIL
- SALT AND BLACK PEPPER TO TASTE

FOR THE HONEY MUSTARD DRESSING:
- 2 TBSP DIJON MUSTARD
- 2 TBSP HONEY
- 2 TBSP APPLE CIDER VINEGAR
- 1/4 CUP EXTRA-VIRGIN OLIVE OIL
- SALT AND BLACK PEPPER TO TASTE

INSTRUCTIONS:
1. PREHEAT THE GRILL TO MEDIUM-HIGH HEAT.
2. SEASON THE CHICKEN BREASTS WITH SALT AND BLACK PEPPER. GRILL THE CHICKEN FOR 6-7 MINUTES PER SIDE OR UNTIL COOKED THROUGH. SET ASIDE TO COOL.
3. BRUSH THE PEACH HALVES WITH OLIVE OIL AND GRILL THEM FOR 2-3 MINUTES PER SIDE OR UNTIL GRILL MARKS APPEAR. SET ASIDE TO COOL.
4. TO MAKE THE HONEY MUSTARD DRESSING, WHISK TOGETHER THE DIJON MUSTARD, HONEY, APPLE CIDER VINEGAR, OLIVE OIL, SALT, AND BLACK PEPPER IN A SMALL BOWL.
5. ONCE THE CHICKEN AND PEACHES HAVE COOLED, SLICE THE CHICKEN INTO THIN STRIPS AND CHOP THE PEACHES INTO BITE-SIZED PIECES.
6. IN A LARGE BOWL, TOSS TOGETHER THE MIXED GREENS, CHERRY TOMATOES, GOAT CHEESE, SLIVERED ALMONDS, CHOPPED BASIL, AND SLICED CHICKEN.
7. DRIZZLE THE HONEY MUSTARD DRESSING OVER THE SALAD AND TOSS TO COAT.
8. TOP THE SALAD WITH THE GRILLED PEACHES AND SERVE.

THIS GRILLED PEACH AND CHICKEN SALAD WITH HONEY MUSTARD DRESSING IS A DELICIOUS AND REFRESHING LUNCH DISH THAT'S PERFECT FOR A HOT SUMMER DAY. THE GRILLED CHICKEN PROVIDES A GOOD SOURCE OF PROTEIN WHILE THE MIXED GREENS, CHERRY TOMATOES, AND GRILLED PEACHES ADD A VARIETY OF VITAMINS, MINERALS, AND ANTIOXIDANTS. THE GOAT CHEESE AND SLIVERED ALMONDS ADD A CRUNCHY AND CREAMY TEXTURE TO THE SALAD WHILE THE HONEY MUSTARD DRESSING ADDS A SWEET AND TANGY FLAVOUR. THIS LUNCH DISH IS NOT ONLY HEALTHY BUT ALSO FLAVOURFUL AND SATISFYING.

SESAME GINGER TOFU BOWL

INGREDIENTS:
- 1 BLOCK EXTRA-FIRM TOFU, DRAINED AND PRESSED
- 2 CUPS COOKED BROWN RICE
- 2 CUPS CHOPPED BROCCOLI
- 1 RED BELL PEPPER, THINLY SLICED
- 1 CARROT, JULIENNED
- 1/4 CUP SLICED SCALLIONS
- 2 TBSP SESAME OIL
- 2 TBSP LOW-SODIUM SOY SAUCE
- 1 TBSP RICE VINEGAR
- 1 TBSP HONEY
- 1 TBSP FRESHLY GRATED GINGER
- 1 GARLIC CLOVE, MINCED
- 1 TBSP SESAME SEEDS
- SALT AND BLACK PEPPER TO TASTE

INSTRUCTIONS:
1. PREHEAT THE OVEN TO 375°F (190°C). CUT THE TOFU INTO 1-INCH CUBES AND PLACE THEM ON A BAKING SHEET LINED WITH PARCHMENT PAPER. BAKE FOR 20-25 MINUTES, FLIPPING HALFWAY THROUGH, UNTIL CRISPY AND GOLDEN BROWN.
2. IN A SMALL BOWL, WHISK TOGETHER THE SESAME OIL, SOY SAUCE, RICE VINEGAR, HONEY, GINGER, GARLIC, AND SESAME SEEDS.
3. IN A LARGE SKILLET, HEAT 1 TBSP OF SESAME OIL OVER MEDIUM-HIGH HEAT. ADD THE BROCCOLI AND COOK FOR 5-6 MINUTES UNTIL TENDER BUT STILL CRISP. ADD THE RED BELL PEPPER AND CARROT AND COOK FOR ANOTHER 2-3 MINUTES UNTIL THE VEGETABLES ARE TENDER.
4. ADD THE COOKED BROWN RICE TO THE SKILLET AND TOSS TO COMBINE WITH THE VEGETABLES.
5. DRIZZLE THE SESAME GINGER SAUCE OVER THE TOFU AND TOSS TO COAT.
6. DIVIDE THE RICE AND VEGETABLE MIXTURE INTO TWO BOWLS. TOP EACH BOWL WITH THE SESAME GINGER TOFU AND SLICED SCALLIONS. SEASON WITH SALT AND BLACK PEPPER TO TASTE.

THIS SESAME GINGER TOFU BOWL IS A HEALTHY AND FLAVOURFUL LUNCH DISH THAT'S PERFECT FOR A VEGETARIAN OR VEGAN DIET. THE TOFU PROVIDES A GOOD SOURCE OF PLANT-BASED PROTEIN WHILE THE BROWN RICE AND VEGETABLES OFFER A VARIETY OF VITAMINS, MINERALS, AND FIBRE. THE SESAME GINGER SAUCE ADDS A SWEET AND SAVOURY FLAVOUR TO THE DISH, AND THE CRISPY BAKED TOFU ADDS A NICE TEXTURE CONTRAST. THIS LUNCH DISH IS NOT ONLY NUTRITIOUS BUT ALSO DELICIOUS AND SATISFYING

MEDITERRANEAN QUINOA SALAD

INGREDIENTS:
- 1 CUP QUINOA, RINSED AND DRAINED
- 2 CUPS VEGETABLE BROTH
- 1 CAN CHICKPEAS, RINSED AND DRAINED
- 1/2 CUP CHOPPED RED ONION
- 1/2 CUP DICED CUCUMBER
- 1/2 CUP DICED TOMATO
- 1/2 CUP CRUMBLED FETA CHEESE
- 1/4 CUP CHOPPED FRESH PARSLEY
- 1/4 CUP CHOPPED FRESH MINT
- 1/4 CUP EXTRA-VIRGIN OLIVE OIL
- 2 TBSP FRESHLY SQUEEZED LEMON JUICE
- 1 TBSP RED WINE VINEGAR
- 1 GARLIC CLOVE, MINCED
- SALT AND BLACK PEPPER TO TASTE

INSTRUCTIONS:
1. IN A MEDIUM SAUCEPAN, BRING THE QUINOA AND VEGETABLE BROTH TO A BOIL. REDUCE THE HEAT TO LOW, COVER, AND SIMMER FOR 15-20 MINUTES UNTIL THE LIQUID IS ABSORBED AND THE QUINOA IS TENDER. REMOVE FROM HEAT AND LET COOL.
2. IN A LARGE BOWL, COMBINE THE COOKED QUINOA, CHICKPEAS, RED ONION, CUCUMBER, TOMATO, FETA CHEESE, PARSLEY, AND MINT.
3. IN A SMALL BOWL, WHISK TOGETHER THE OLIVE OIL, LEMON JUICE, RED WINE VINEGAR, GARLIC, SALT, AND BLACK PEPPER.
4. POUR THE DRESSING OVER THE QUINOA SALAD AND TOSS TO COMBINE.
5. SERVE THE SALAD AT ROOM TEMPERATURE OR CHILLED.

THIS MEDITERRANEAN QUINOA SALAD IS PACKED WITH FLAVOUR AND NUTRITION. THE QUINOA AND CHICKPEAS PROVIDE PLANT-BASED PROTEIN AND FIBRE WHILE THE FRESH VEGETABLES AND HERBS OFFER A VARIETY OF VITAMINS AND MINERALS. THE FETA CHEESE ADDS A TANGY AND SALTY FLAVOUR, AND THE DRESSING MADE WITH OLIVE OIL, LEMON JUICE, AND GARLIC ADDS A ZESTY AND REFRESHING TASTE. THIS SALAD IS PERFECT FOR A LIGHT AND HEALTHY LUNCH AND CAN ALSO BE PREPARED AHEAD OF TIME FOR MEAL PREP.

SPICED LENTIL AND PUMPKIN STEW

INGREDIENTS:
- 1 CUP RED LENTILS
- 3 CUPS WATER
- 1 SMALL PUMPKIN, PEELED AND CUBED (ABOUT 2 CUPS)
- 1 LARGE ONION, CHOPPED
- 2 GARLIC CLOVES, MINCED
- 1 TBSP GRATED GINGER
- 1 TSP GROUND CUMIN
- 1 TSP GROUND CORIANDER
- 1/2 TSP GROUND CINNAMON
- 1/2 TSP GROUND TURMERIC
- 1/4 TSP CAYENNE PEPPER
- 2 TBSP OLIVE OIL
- SALT AND BLACK PEPPER TO TASTE
- FRESH CILANTRO, CHOPPED, FOR GARNISH

INSTRUCTIONS:
1. RINSE THE LENTILS IN COLD WATER AND DRAIN WELL. IN A MEDIUM SAUCEPAN, BRING THE WATER TO A BOIL AND ADD THE LENTILS. REDUCE THE HEAT TO LOW AND SIMMER FOR 15-20 MINUTES UNTIL THE LENTILS ARE TENDER AND THE WATER HAS BEEN ABSORBED.
2. IN A LARGE POT, HEAT THE OLIVE OIL OVER MEDIUM-HIGH HEAT. ADD THE ONION, GARLIC, AND GINGER AND SAUTÉ FOR 5 MINUTES UNTIL THE ONION IS SOFT AND TRANSLUCENT.
3. ADD THE CUBED PUMPKIN, CUMIN, CORIANDER, CINNAMON, TURMERIC, AND CAYENNE PEPPER TO THE POT. STIR WELL TO COAT THE PUMPKIN WITH THE SPICES AND COOK FOR ANOTHER 5 MINUTES.
4. ADD THE COOKED LENTILS TO THE POT AND STIR TO COMBINE. SEASON WITH SALT AND BLACK PEPPER TO TASTE.
5. COVER THE POT AND SIMMER THE STEW FOR 15-20 MINUTES UNTIL THE PUMPKIN IS TENDER AND THE FLAVOURS HAVE MELDED TOGETHER.
6. SERVE THE STEW HOT, GARNISHED WITH FRESH CILANTRO.

THIS SPICED LENTIL AND PUMPKIN STEW IS A DELICIOUS AND HEARTY VEGAN MEAL THAT'S FULL OF FLAVOUR AND NUTRITION. THE RED LENTILS ARE A GREAT SOURCE OF PLANT-BASED PROTEIN AND FIBRE, WHILE THE PUMPKIN ADDS SWEETNESS AND CREAMINESS TO THE STEW. THE SPICES USED IN THE RECIPE, SUCH AS CUMIN, CORIANDER, AND CINNAMON, PROVIDE A WARM AND FRAGRANT AROMA, AND THE CAYENNE PEPPER ADDS A BIT OF HEAT. THIS RECIPE IS PERFECT FOR A CHILLY DAY AND CAN BE ENJOYED AS A MAIN DISH OR A SIDE DISH.

QUINOA SUSHI ROLLS WITH AVOCADO AND MANGO

INGREDIENTS:
- 1 CUP QUINOA, RINSED AND DRAINED
- 2 CUPS WATER
- 3 TBSP RICE VINEGAR
- 1 TBSP HONEY
- 1/2 TSP SALT
- 4 SHEETS OF NORI
- 1 RIPE AVOCADO, THINLY SLICED
- 1 SMALL MANGO, THINLY SLICED
- 1 SMALL CUCUMBER, THINLY SLICED
- 1 SMALL RED BELL PEPPER, THINLY SLICED
- 1 SMALL CARROT, THINLY SLICED
- 1 TBSP BLACK SESAME SEEDS
- SOY SAUCE AND WASABI, FOR SERVING

INSTRUCTIONS:
1. IN A MEDIUM SAUCEPAN, BRING THE QUINOA AND WATER TO A BOIL. REDUCE THE HEAT TO LOW AND SIMMER, COVERED, FOR 15-20 MINUTES UNTIL THE QUINOA IS TENDER AND THE WATER HAS BEEN ABSORBED.
2. IN A SMALL BOWL, WHISK TOGETHER THE RICE VINEGAR, HONEY, AND SALT. ONCE THE QUINOA IS COOKED, REMOVE IT FROM THE HEAT AND LET IT COOL SLIGHTLY. ADD THE VINEGAR MIXTURE TO THE QUINOA AND STIR WELL TO COMBINE.
3. PLACE A SHEET OF NORI (DRIED EDIBLE SEAWEED) ON A CLEAN WORK SURFACE, SHINY SIDE DOWN. USING A SPOON, SPREAD A LAYER OF QUINOA OVER THE NORI, LEAVING A 1-INCH BORDER AT THE TOP EDGE.
4. ARRANGE A LAYER OF AVOCADO, MANGO, CUCUMBER, BELL PEPPER, AND CARROT ON TOP OF THE QUINOA. SPRINKLE WITH BLACK SESAME SEEDS.
5. STARTING AT THE BOTTOM EDGE, TIGHTLY ROLL UP THE NORI AND FILLING INTO A CYLINDER, PRESSING THE ROLL TOGETHER AS YOU GO. WET THE TOP BORDER WITH A BIT OF WATER TO SEAL THE ROLL.
6. REPEAT WITH THE REMAINING SHEETS OF NORI AND FILLING.
7. USING A SHARP KNIFE, SLICE EACH ROLL INTO 6-8 PIECES.
8. SERVE THE SUSHI ROLLS WITH SOY SAUCE AND WASABI ON THE SIDE.

THESE QUINOA SUSHI ROLLS ARE A FUN AND HEALTHY TWIST ON TRADITIONAL SUSHI, WITH A VIBRANT MIX OF COLOURS, TEXTURES, AND FLAVOURS. THE QUINOA ADDS A NUTTY AND SLIGHTLY CRUNCHY TEXTURE, WHILE THE AVOCADO AND MANGO BRING CREAMINESS AND SWEETNESS. THE VEGETABLES ADD A REFRESHING CRUNCH AND A POP OF COLOUR, AND THE BLACK SESAME SEEDS PROVIDE A SUBTLE NUTTY FLAVOUR AND VISUAL CONTRAST. THIS RECIPE IS PERFECT FOR A LIGHT AND SATISFYING LUNCH OR A FUN AND HEALTHY APPETISER.

BEETROOT AND LENTIL SALAD WITH FETA AND WALNUTS

INGREDIENTS:

- 2 MEDIUM BEETROOTS, COOKED AND DICED
- 1 CUP COOKED GREEN LENTILS
- 2 CUPS MIXED SALAD GREENS
- 1/2 CUP CRUMBLED FETA CHEESE
- 1/2 CUP CHOPPED WALNUTS
- 1/4 CUP CHOPPED FRESH PARSLEY
- 2 TBSP OLIVE OIL
- 2 TBSP RED WINE VINEGAR
- 1 TSP DIJON MUSTARD
- SALT AND PEPPER TO TASTE

INSTRUCTIONS:

1. IN A LARGE BOWL, COMBINE THE DICED BEETROOT, COOKED LENTILS, AND MIXED SALAD GREENS.
2. IN A SEPARATE BOWL, WHISK TOGETHER THE OLIVE OIL, RED WINE VINEGAR, DIJON MUSTARD, SALT, AND PEPPER TO MAKE A VINAIGRETTE.
3. POUR THE VINAIGRETTE OVER THE SALAD AND TOSS TO COAT.
4. TOP THE SALAD WITH CRUMBLED FETA CHEESE, CHOPPED WALNUTS, AND FRESH PARSLEY.

THIS SALAD IS PACKED WITH NUTRITIOUS INGREDIENTS, INCLUDING THE ANTIOXIDANT-RICH BEETROOT AND PROTEIN-PACKED LENTILS. THE FETA CHEESE AND WALNUTS ADD A SATISFYING CRUNCH AND A SALTY CONTRAST TO THE SWEET BEETS, WHILE THE FRESH PARSLEY ADDS A BURST OF FRESHNESS. THE SIMPLE VINAIGRETTE TIES EVERYTHING TOGETHER WITH A TANGY AND SAVOURY FLAVOUR. THIS SALAD IS PERFECT FOR A LIGHT AND HEALTHY LUNCH, AND CAN BE PREPARED AHEAD OF TIME FOR AN EASY AND CONVENIENT MEAL.

SUSHI-INSPIRED QUINOA BOWL

INGREDIENTS:
- 1 CUP QUINOA, RINSED AND DRAINED
- 2 CUPS WATER
- 2 TBSP RICE VINEGAR
- 1 TBSP HONEY
- 1 TSP SESAME OIL
- 1/4 TSP SALT
- 1/4 CUP CHOPPED CUCUMBER
- 1/4 CUP SHREDDED CARROTS
- 1/4 CUP SLICED AVOCADO
- 1/4 CUP SLICED RADISH
- 1/4 CUP CHOPPED SCALLIONS
- 1/2 CUP EDAMAME BEANS
- 1/2 CUP COOKED SHRIMP OR IMITATION CRAB MEAT
- 1 TBSP PICKLED GINGER
- 1 TBSP SESAME SEEDS

INSTRUCTIONS:
1. IN A MEDIUM SAUCEPAN, COMBINE THE QUINOA AND WATER AND BRING TO A BOIL OVER HIGH HEAT. REDUCE THE HEAT TO LOW AND SIMMER, COVERED, FOR 15-20 MINUTES OR UNTIL THE QUINOA IS TENDER AND THE WATER HAS BEEN ABSORBED.
2. IN A SMALL BOWL, WHISK TOGETHER THE RICE VINEGAR, HONEY, SESAME OIL, AND SALT TO MAKE A DRESSING.
3. FLUFF THE QUINOA WITH A FORK AND STIR IN THE DRESSING.
4. DIVIDE THE QUINOA BETWEEN TWO BOWLS AND TOP WITH CUCUMBER, CARROTS, AVOCADO, RADISH, SCALLIONS, EDAMAME BEANS, AND COOKED SHRIMP OR IMITATION CRAB MEAT.
5. GARNISH EACH BOWL WITH PICKLED GINGER AND SESAME SEEDS.

THIS SUSHI-INSPIRED QUINOA BOWL IS A HEALTHY AND FLAVOURFUL ALTERNATIVE TO TRADITIONAL SUSHI ROLLS. THE QUINOA PROVIDES A HEARTY BASE AND IS SEASONED WITH A TANGY AND SLIGHTLY SWEET DRESSING. THE FRESH VEGETABLES AND PROTEIN-RICH EDAMAME AND SHRIMP OR CRAB MEAT ADD TEXTURE AND FLAVOUR, WHILE THE PICKLED GINGER AND SESAME SEEDS PROVIDE A UNIQUE TWIST ON TRADITIONAL SUSHI FLAVOURS. THIS DISH IS PERFECT FOR A LIGHT AND HEALTHY LUNCH, AND CAN BE EASILY CUSTOMIZED WITH YOUR FAVOURITE SUSHI INGREDIENTS.

SPICY LENTIL AND SQUASH STEW

INGREDIENTS:

- 1 CUP DRIED RED LENTILS
- 1 SMALL BUTTERNUT SQUASH, PEELED AND CUBED
- 1 CAN OF COCONUT MILK
- 1 TABLESPOON COCONUT OIL
- 1 ONION, CHOPPED
- 3 CLOVES OF GARLIC, MINCED
- 1 TABLESPOON GRATED FRESH GINGER
- 1 TEASPOON GROUND CUMIN
- 1 TEASPOON GROUND CORIANDER
- 1 TEASPOON PAPRIKA
- 1/2 TEASPOON CAYENNE PEPPER
- SALT AND PEPPER TO TASTE
- FRESH CILANTRO LEAVES FOR GARNISH

INSTRUCTIONS:

1. RINSE THE LENTILS IN COLD WATER AND DRAIN.
2. HEAT THE COCONUT OIL IN A LARGE POT OVER MEDIUM HEAT. ADD THE ONION AND COOK UNTIL TRANSLUCENT, STIRRING OCCASIONALLY.
3. ADD THE GARLIC, GINGER, CUMIN, CORIANDER, PAPRIKA, AND CAYENNE PEPPER. STIR TO COMBINE AND COOK FOR 1-2 MINUTES UNTIL FRAGRANT.
4. ADD THE LENTILS, BUTTERNUT SQUASH, AND COCONUT MILK. STIR TO COMBINE AND BRING TO A BOIL.
5. REDUCE HEAT TO LOW, COVER THE POT, AND SIMMER FOR 20-25 MINUTES OR UNTIL THE LENTILS AND SQUASH ARE TENDER AND THE STEW HAS THICKENED.
6. SEASON WITH SALT AND PEPPER TO TASTE.
7. SERVE HOT, GARNISHED WITH FRESH CILANTRO LEAVES.

THIS HEARTY AND FLAVOURFUL STEW IS PACKED WITH PROTEIN AND FIBRE FROM THE LENTILS AND NUTRIENTS FROM THE BUTTERNUT SQUASH. THE COCONUT MILK ADDS CREAMINESS AND A TOUCH OF SWEETNESS, WHILE THE SPICES GIVE IT A KICK OF HEAT. IT'S A PERFECT LUNCH OR DINNER OPTION THAT IS BOTH HEALTHY AND TASTY.

BEETROOT AND CHICKPEA SALAD WITH ORANGE VINAIGRETTE

INGREDIENTS:

- 2 MEDIUM-SIZED BEETROOTS, PEELED AND DICED
- 1 CAN CHICKPEAS, DRAINED AND RINSED
- 2 CUPS BABY SPINACH LEAVES
- 1 ORANGE, JUICED
- 1 TBSP HONEY
- 2 TBSP OLIVE OIL
- 1/4 TSP GROUND CUMIN
- SALT AND PEPPER TO TASTE
- 1/4 CUP CHOPPED FRESH PARSLEY

INSTRUCTIONS:

1. PREHEAT OVEN TO 400°F. SPREAD THE DICED BEETROOT ON A BAKING SHEET AND ROAST FOR 20-25 MINUTES OR UNTIL TENDER.
2. IN A LARGE BOWL, MIX TOGETHER THE ROASTED BEETROOT, CHICKPEAS, AND BABY SPINACH LEAVES.
3. IN A SEPARATE SMALL BOWL, WHISK TOGETHER THE ORANGE JUICE, HONEY, OLIVE OIL, CUMIN, SALT, AND PEPPER TO MAKE THE DRESSING.
4. DRIZZLE THE DRESSING OVER THE BEETROOT AND CHICKPEA MIXTURE AND TOSS TO COMBINE.
5. GARNISH THE SALAD WITH CHOPPED PARSLEY BEFORE SERVING.

THIS SALAD IS PACKED WITH NUTRIENTS FROM THE BEETROOTS AND CHICKPEAS, AND THE ORANGE VINAIGRETTE ADDS A REFRESHING AND TANGY FLAVOR.

MEDITERRANEAN LAMB AND QUINOA BOWL

INGREDIENTS:

- 1 POUND LAMB LEG MEAT, TRIMMED AND CUT INTO 1-INCH PIECES
- 1 CUP QUINOA, RINSED
- 1 RED BELL PEPPER, DICED
- 1 ZUCCHINI, DICED
- 1/2 RED ONION, SLICED
- 2 CLOVES GARLIC, MINCED
- 2 TBSP OLIVE OIL
- 1 TBSP LEMON JUICE
- 1 TSP DRIED OREGANO
- SALT AND PEPPER TO TASTE
- 1/4 CUP CRUMBLED FETA CHEESE
- FRESH PARSLEY FOR GARNISH

INSTRUCTIONS:

1. IN A LARGE BOWL, COMBINE THE LAMB, OLIVE OIL, LEMON JUICE, OREGANO, SALT, AND PEPPER. MARINATE FOR AT LEAST 30 MINUTES.
2. PREHEAT OVEN TO 400°F. SPREAD THE MARINATED LAMB OUT ON A BAKING SHEET AND BAKE FOR 15-20 MINUTES, OR UNTIL COOKED THROUGH.
3. MEANWHILE, COOK THE QUINOA ACCORDING TO PACKAGE INSTRUCTIONS.
4. IN A LARGE SKILLET, SAUTÉ THE RED BELL PEPPER, ZUCCHINI, RED ONION, AND GARLIC UNTIL TENDER.
5. TO ASSEMBLE THE BOWLS, DIVIDE THE COOKED QUINOA AMONG FOUR BOWLS. TOP WITH THE SAUTÉED VEGETABLES, BAKED LAMB, AND CRUMBLED FETA CHEESE. GARNISH WITH FRESH PARSLEY.

THIS MEDITERRANEAN-INSPIRED LAMB AND QUINOA BOWL IS A HEALTHY AND SATISFYING MEAL THAT IS PACKED WITH PROTEIN AND NUTRITIOUS VEGETABLES. THE LEMON AND OREGANO MARINADE ADDS A DELICIOUS FLAVOUR TO THE LAMB, WHILE THE FETA CHEESE ADDS A TANGY AND CREAMY FINISH TO THE DISH

POACHED COD WITH GINGER AND SHIITAKE MUSHROOMS

INGREDIENTS:

- 4 COD FILLETS, SKIN REMOVED
- 1 CUP SHIITAKE MUSHROOMS, SLICED
- 2 CLOVES GARLIC, MINCED
- 1 TBSP FRESH GINGER, GRATED
- 2 CUPS LOW-SODIUM CHICKEN OR VEGETABLE BROTH
- 2 TBSP LOW-SODIUM SOY SAUCE
- 1 TBSP RICE VINEGAR
- 1 TBSP SESAME OIL
- 2 GREEN ONIONS, SLICED
- SALT AND PEPPER TO TASTE

INSTRUCTIONS:

1. IN A LARGE SKILLET, SAUTÉ THE SHIITAKE MUSHROOMS, GARLIC, AND GINGER UNTIL TENDER.
2. ADD THE BROTH, SOY SAUCE, RICE VINEGAR, SESAME OIL, AND GREEN ONIONS TO THE SKILLET. BRING TO A BOIL, THEN REDUCE HEAT TO LOW AND LET SIMMER FOR 5-10 MINUTES.
3. SEASON THE COD FILLETS WITH SALT AND PEPPER, THEN ADD THEM TO THE SKILLET. COVER AND SIMMER FOR 7-10 MINUTES, OR UNTIL THE FISH IS COOKED THROUGH AND FLAKES EASILY WITH A FORK.
4. SERVE THE POACHED COD WITH THE MUSHROOM AND GINGER BROTH SPOONED OVER THE TOP.

THIS POACHED COD WITH GINGER AND SHIITAKE MUSHROOMS IS A HEALTHY AND FLAVOURFUL DISH THAT IS PACKED WITH PROTEIN AND NUTRIENTS. THE GINGER AND MUSHROOMS ADD A DELICIOUS UMAMI FLAVOUR TO THE DISH, WHILE THE POACHING METHOD KEEPS THE FISH MOIST AND TENDER

CHICKPEA AND SPINACH CURRY WITH COCONUT MILK

INGREDIENTS:

- 2 CANS CHICKPEAS, DRAINED AND RINSED
- 1 ONION, DICED
- 2 CLOVES GARLIC, MINCED
- 2 TBSP GINGER, GRATED
- 2 TBSP VEGETABLE OIL
- 1 TBSP CURRY POWDER
- 1 TSP GROUND CUMIN
- 1 TSP GROUND CORIANDER
- 1/2 TSP GROUND TURMERIC
- 1/4 TSP CAYENNE PEPPER
- 1 CAN COCONUT MILK
- 1 CUP VEGETABLE BROTH
- 1 BUNCH SPINACH, STEMMED AND CHOPPED
- SALT AND PEPPER TO TASTE
- COOKED RICE FOR SERVING

INSTRUCTIONS:

1. IN A LARGE SKILLET, SAUTÉ THE ONION, GARLIC, AND GINGER IN THE VEGETABLE OIL UNTIL TENDER.
2. ADD THE CURRY POWDER, CUMIN, CORIANDER, TURMERIC, AND CAYENNE PEPPER TO THE SKILLET. COOK FOR 1-2 MINUTES, OR UNTIL FRAGRANT.
3. ADD THE CHICKPEAS, COCONUT MILK, AND VEGETABLE BROTH TO THE SKILLET. STIR TO COMBINE.
4. SIMMER THE MIXTURE FOR 10-15 MINUTES, OR UNTIL THE SAUCE HAS THICKENED AND THE CHICKPEAS ARE HEATED THROUGH.
5. ADD THE CHOPPED SPINACH TO THE SKILLET AND STIR UNTIL WILTED. SEASON WITH SALT AND PEPPER TO TASTE.
6. SERVE THE CHICKPEA AND SPINACH CURRY OVER COOKED RICE.

THIS VEGETARIAN CURRY IS A FILLING AND SATISFYING DISH THAT IS PACKED WITH PROTEIN, FIBRE, AND HEALTHY FATS FROM THE CHICKPEAS AND COCONUT MILK. THE SPINACH ADDS A NUTRITIOUS BOOST OF VITAMINS AND MINERALS, WHILE THE SPICES AND AROMATICS CREATE A DELICIOUS AND WARMING FLAVOUR.

MUSHROOM AND LENTIL SHEPHERD'S PIE: PART 1.

INGREDIENTS FOR THE FILLING:

- 2 TBSP OLIVE OIL
- 1 ONION, DICED
- 3 CLOVES GARLIC, MINCED
- 1 LB MUSHROOMS, SLICED
- 2 CUPS COOKED GREEN OR BROWN LENTILS
- 1 TBSP TOMATO PASTE
- 1 TBSP SOY SAUCE
- 1 TSP DRIED THYME
- 1 TSP SMOKED PAPRIKA
- 1/2 TSP SALT
- 1/4 TSP BLACK PEPPER
- 1/2 CUP VEGETABLE BROTH

INGREDIENTS FOR THE TOPPING:

- 2 POUNDS RUSSET POTATOES, PEELED AND CUT INTO CHUNKS
- 2 TBSP UNSALTED BUTTER
- 1/4 CUP MILK
- SALT AND PEPPER TO TASTE

INSTRUCTIONS: PART 2.

1. PREHEAT OVEN TO 375°F.
2. TO MAKE THE FILLING, HEAT THE OLIVE OIL IN A LARGE SKILLET OVER MEDIUM HEAT. ADD THE ONION AND GARLIC AND SAUTÉ UNTIL THE ONION IS TRANSLUCENT, ABOUT 5-7 MINUTES.
3. ADD THE MUSHROOMS TO THE SKILLET AND SAUTÉ UNTIL THEY RELEASE THEIR LIQUID AND START TO BROWN, ABOUT 10 MINUTES.
4. ADD THE COOKED LENTILS, TOMATO PASTE, SOY SAUCE, THYME, SMOKED PAPRIKA, SALT, PEPPER, AND VEGETABLE BROTH TO THE SKILLET. STIR TO COMBINE AND COOK UNTIL THE MIXTURE IS HEATED THROUGH, ABOUT 5 MINUTES.
5. TO MAKE THE TOPPING, PLACE THE POTATOES IN A LARGE POT OF SALTED WATER AND BRING TO A BOIL. REDUCE HEAT TO MEDIUM-LOW AND SIMMER UNTIL THE POTATOES ARE TENDER, ABOUT 15-20 MINUTES.
6. DRAIN THE POTATOES AND RETURN THEM TO THE POT. ADD THE BUTTER, MILK, SALT, AND PEPPER. MASH THE POTATOES UNTIL SMOOTH.
7. TO ASSEMBLE THE SHEPHERD'S PIE, SPREAD THE LENTIL AND MUSHROOM MIXTURE INTO A 9X13 INCH BAKING DISH. SPOON THE MASHED POTATOES OVER THE TOP AND SMOOTH OUT WITH A SPATULA.
8. BAKE THE SHEPHERD'S PIE FOR 25-30 MINUTES, OR UNTIL THE TOP IS GOLDEN BROWN AND THE FILLING IS HEATED THROUGH.

THIS MUSHROOM AND LENTIL SHEPHERD'S PIE IS A HEARTY AND SATISFYING DISH THAT IS PERFECT FOR A COMFORTING WEEKNIGHT MEAL. THE LENTILS AND MUSHROOMS ADD A MEATY TEXTURE AND FLAVOUR TO THE DISH, WHILE THE MASHED POTATO TOPPING IS CREAMY AND DELICIOUS. ENJOY!

SAVOURY SPINACH AND FETA QUICHE WITH ALMOND FLOUR CRUST

INGREDIENTS:
- 1 1/2 CUPS ALMOND FLOUR
- 1/4 CUP MELTED BUTTER
- 1/4 TEASPOON SALT
- 1/4 TEASPOON BLACK PEPPER
- 5 LARGE EGGS
- 1/2 CUP MILK
- 1/2 CUP CRUMBLED FETA CHEESE
- 1/2 CUP CHOPPED SPINACH
- 1/4 CUP DICED ONION
- 1/4 TEASPOON GARLIC POWDER
- 1/4 TEASPOON DRIED THYME

INSTRUCTIONS:
1. PREHEAT THE OVEN TO 350°F.
2. IN A MIXING BOWL, COMBINE THE ALMOND FLOUR, MELTED BUTTER, SALT, AND PEPPER. MIX UNTIL THE INGREDIENTS ARE WELL COMBINED.
3. PRESS THE MIXTURE INTO THE BOTTOM AND UP THE SIDES OF A 9-INCH PIE DISH. BAKE IN THE OVEN FOR 10-12 MINUTES OR UNTIL THE CRUST IS LIGHTLY GOLDEN.
4. IN A SEPARATE MIXING BOWL, WHISK TOGETHER THE EGGS AND MILK. ADD THE FETA CHEESE, SPINACH, ONION, GARLIC POWDER, AND DRIED THYME. MIX UNTIL THE INGREDIENTS ARE WELL COMBINED.
5. POUR THE MIXTURE INTO THE ALMOND FLOUR CRUST. BAKE IN THE OVEN FOR 25-30 MINUTES OR UNTIL THE QUICHE IS SET AND THE TOP IS LIGHTLY GOLDEN.
6. REMOVE FROM THE OVEN AND LET COOL FOR 5-10 MINUTES BEFORE SLICING AND SERVING.

THIS SAVOURY SPINACH AND FETA QUICHE WITH ALMOND FLOUR CRUST IS A DELICIOUS AND HEALTHY ALTERNATIVE TO TRADITIONAL QUICHES. THE ALMOND FLOUR CRUST IS GLUTEN-FREE AND ADDS A NUTTY FLAVOUR TO THE DISH, WHILE THE SPINACH AND FETA CHEESE ADD A SAVOURY AND TANGY TWIST. THE EGGS PROVIDE A GOOD SOURCE OF PROTEIN AND NUTRIENTS, AND THE THYME AND GARLIC POWDER ADD AN HERBACEOUS AND AROMATIC FLAVOUR. ENJOY!

BAKED VEGETABLE FRITTATA WITH SWEET POTATO CRUST

INGREDIENTS:
- 1 MEDIUM SWEET POTATO, PEELED AND GRATED
- 2 TABLESPOONS OLIVE OIL
- 1 SMALL ONION, DICED
- 1 RED BELL PEPPER, DICED
- 1 ZUCCHINI, SLICED
- 1 CUP CHERRY TOMATOES, HALVED
- 6 LARGE EGGS
- 1/4 CUP MILK
- 1/4 CUP FRESH BASIL, CHOPPED
- SALT AND PEPPER TO TASTE

INSTRUCTIONS:
1. PREHEAT THE OVEN TO 375°F.
2. IN A LARGE OVEN-SAFE SKILLET, HEAT 1 TABLESPOON OF OLIVE OIL OVER MEDIUM HEAT. ADD THE GRATED SWEET POTATO AND COOK FOR 5-7 MINUTES OR UNTIL THE SWEET POTATO IS TENDER AND LIGHTLY BROWNED. REMOVE THE SKILLET FROM THE HEAT.
3. IN A SEPARATE SKILLET, HEAT THE REMAINING TABLESPOON OF OLIVE OIL OVER MEDIUM HEAT. ADD THE ONION, RED BELL PEPPER, AND ZUCCHINI. COOK FOR 5-7 MINUTES OR UNTIL THE VEGETABLES ARE TENDER. ADD THE CHERRY TOMATOES AND COOK FOR AN ADDITIONAL 2-3 MINUTES OR UNTIL THE TOMATOES HAVE SOFTENED.
4. IN A MIXING BOWL, WHISK TOGETHER THE EGGS, MILK, AND CHOPPED BASIL. SEASON WITH SALT AND PEPPER TO TASTE.
5. POUR THE EGG MIXTURE OVER THE SWEET POTATO CRUST IN THE OVEN-SAFE SKILLET. ADD THE SAUTÉED VEGETABLES ON TOP OF THE EGG MIXTURE.
6. BAKE IN THE OVEN FOR 20-25 MINUTES OR UNTIL THE FRITTATA IS SET AND THE TOP IS LIGHTLY BROWNED.
7. REMOVE FROM THE OVEN AND LET COOL FOR 5-10 MINUTES BEFORE SLICING AND SERVING.

THIS VEGETABLE FRITTATA WITH SWEET POTATO CRUST IS A DELICIOUS AND HEALTHY ALTERNATIVE TO TRADITIONAL BREAKFAST DISHES. THE SWEET POTATO CRUST ADDS A NUTRITIOUS AND TASTY TWIST, WHILE THE VEGETABLES ADD COLOUR AND FLAVOUR. THE EGGS PROVIDE A GOOD SOURCE OF PROTEIN AND NUTRIENTS, AND THE FRESH BASIL ADDS A POP OF HERBACEOUS FLAVOUR. ENJOY!

ASIAN BEEF AND VEGETABLE STIR FRY WITH CAULIFLOWER RICE

INGREDIENTS:
- 1 LB. LEAN BEEF, SLICED INTO THIN STRIPS
- 2 CUPS BROCCOLI FLORETS
- 1 RED BELL PEPPER, SLICED
- 1 CUP SNAP PEAS
- 1 SMALL ONION, SLICED
- 2 CLOVES GARLIC, MINCED
- 1 TABLESPOON GINGER, GRATED
- 2 TABLESPOONS SOY SAUCE
- 2 TABLESPOONS RICE VINEGAR
- 1 TABLESPOON HONEY
- 1 TABLESPOON SESAME OIL
- 1 TABLESPOON CORN-STARCH
- SALT AND PEPPER TO TASTE
- 1 HEAD OF CAULIFLOWER, RICED

INSTRUCTIONS:
1. IN A SMALL BOWL, WHISK TOGETHER SOY SAUCE, RICE VINEGAR, HONEY, SESAME OIL, CORN-STARCH, AND 1/4 CUP OF WATER.
2. HEAT A LARGE SKILLET OR WOK OVER HIGH HEAT. ADD THE BEEF AND COOK FOR 3-4 MINUTES OR UNTIL BROWNED. REMOVE THE BEEF FROM THE SKILLET AND SET ASIDE.
3. IN THE SAME SKILLET, ADD THE BROCCOLI, RED BELL PEPPER, SNAP PEAS, ONION, GARLIC, AND GINGER. STIR-FRY FOR 5-6 MINUTES OR UNTIL VEGETABLES ARE TENDER-CRISP.
4. ADD THE BEEF BACK INTO THE SKILLET, POUR THE SAUCE OVER THE TOP, AND STIR TO COMBINE. COOK FOR AN ADDITIONAL 2-3 MINUTES OR UNTIL THE SAUCE HAS THICKENED AND THE BEEF IS COOKED THROUGH. SEASON WITH SALT AND PEPPER TO TASTE.
5. MEANWHILE, PREPARE THE CAULIFLOWER RICE. CUT THE HEAD OF CAULIFLOWER INTO FLORETS AND PULSE IN A FOOD PROCESSOR UNTIL IT RESEMBLES RICE.
6. SERVE THE BEEF AND VEGETABLE STIR FRY OVER THE CAULIFLOWER RICE.

THIS DISH IS PACKED WITH PROTEIN AND FIBRE FROM THE LEAN BEEF AND VEGETABLES. THE CAULIFLOWER RICE IS A HEALTHY ALTERNATIVE TO TRADITIONAL RICE, ADDING EXTRA FIBRE AND VITAMINS TO THE DISH. THE SAUCE IS A PERFECT BALANCE OF SWEET AND SAVOURY FLAVOURS WITHOUT BEING LOADED WITH SODIUM OR ADDED SUGARS. ENJOY!

GRILLED PINEAPPLE AND QUINOA SALAD WITH MANGO DRESSING

INGREDIENTS:

- 1/2 FRESH PINEAPPLE, PEELED AND CORED
- 1 CUP QUINOA, RINSED AND DRAINED
- 2 CUPS WATER
- 1/2 CUP RED ONION, FINELY CHOPPED
- 1/2 CUP FRESH CILANTRO, CHOPPED
- 1/4 CUP ROASTED CASHEWS, CHOPPED
- SALT AND PEPPER TO TASTE

FOR THE MANGO DRESSING:

- 1 RIPE MANGO, PEELED AND CHOPPED
- 1/4 CUP OLIVE OIL
- 2 TABLESPOONS LIME JUICE
- 1 TABLESPOON HONEY
- 1/4 TEASPOON CUMIN
- SALT AND PEPPER TO TASTE

INSTRUCTIONS:

1. PREHEAT GRILL OR GRILL PAN TO MEDIUM-HIGH HEAT.
2. CUT THE PINEAPPLE INTO 1/2 INCH SLICES AND GRILL FOR 2-3 MINUTES ON EACH SIDE OR UNTIL LIGHTLY CHARRED. REMOVE FROM GRILL AND LET COOL. ONCE COOLED, CHOP THE PINEAPPLE INTO BITE-SIZED PIECES.
3. IN A MEDIUM POT, COMBINE QUINOA AND WATER. BRING TO A BOIL, REDUCE HEAT, COVER AND SIMMER FOR 15-20 MINUTES OR UNTIL WATER IS ABSORBED AND QUINOA IS TENDER. FLUFF WITH A FORK AND LET COOL.
4. IN A LARGE BOWL, COMBINE CHOPPED PINEAPPLE, COOKED QUINOA, RED ONION, CILANTRO, AND CHOPPED CASHEWS. SEASON WITH SALT AND PEPPER TO TASTE.
5. TO MAKE THE MANGO DRESSING, BLEND THE CHOPPED MANGO, OLIVE OIL, LIME JUICE, HONEY, CUMIN, SALT, AND PEPPER IN A BLENDER UNTIL SMOOTH.
6. POUR THE MANGO DRESSING OVER THE PINEAPPLE AND QUINOA SALAD AND TOSS TO COAT.

THIS SALAD IS A DELICIOUS COMBINATION OF SWEET AND SAVOURY FLAVOURS. GRILLED PINEAPPLE ADDS A SMOKY SWEETNESS TO THE DISH, WHILE THE QUINOA, RED ONION, AND CILANTRO ADD A NICE CRUNCH AND SAVOURY DEPTH. THE ROASTED CASHEWS PROVIDE A NUTTY TEXTURE AND FLAVOUR. THE MANGO DRESSING IS A PERFECT COMPLEMENT TO THE SALAD, ADDING A SWEET AND TANGY FLAVOUR WITH A HINT OF SPICE FROM THE CUMIN. ENJOY!

SPICY SWEET POTATO AND BLACK BEAN BOWL WITH KIMCHI AND COCONUT YOGURT

INGREDIENTS:
- 1 LARGE SWEET POTATO, PEELED AND CUBED
- 1 CAN BLACK BEANS, RINSED AND DRAINED
- 1/2 CUP KIMCHI, CHOPPED
- 1/2 CUP COCONUT YOGURT
- 1 TABLESPOON OLIVE OIL
- 1 TEASPOON SMOKED PAPRIKA
- 1/2 TEASPOON CUMIN
- 1/4 TEASPOON CAYENNE PEPPER
- SALT AND PEPPER TO TASTE
- FRESH CILANTRO FOR GARNISH

INSTRUCTIONS:
1. PREHEAT OVEN TO 400°F (200°C).
2. IN A BOWL, MIX TOGETHER OLIVE OIL, SMOKED PAPRIKA, CUMIN, CAYENNE PEPPER, SALT, AND PEPPER. ADD THE CUBED SWEET POTATO AND TOSS UNTIL EVENLY COATED.
3. SPREAD THE SWEET POTATO CUBES IN A SINGLE LAYER ON A BAKING SHEET AND BAKE FOR 25–30 MINUTES OR UNTIL TENDER AND LIGHTLY BROWNED.
4. IN A SMALL BOWL, MIX TOGETHER THE CHOPPED KIMCHI AND BLACK BEANS.
5. TO ASSEMBLE THE BOWL, START WITH A BASE OF THE SPICY SWEET POTATO CUBES. TOP WITH THE BLACK BEAN AND KIMCHI MIXTURE, AND A DOLLOP OF COCONUT YOGURT. GARNISH WITH FRESH CILANTRO.

THIS DISH IS FULL OF FLAVOUR AND NUTRITION! THE SWEET POTATOES PROVIDE A GOOD SOURCE OF FIBRE, VITAMIN A, AND POTASSIUM. THE BLACK BEANS OFFER PROTEIN, FIBRE, AND A VARIETY OF ESSENTIAL VITAMINS AND MINERALS. KIMCHI IS A FERMENTED FOOD THAT'S LOADED WITH BENEFICIAL BACTERIA FOR GUT HEALTH. COCONUT YOGURT IS A DAIRY-FREE ALTERNATIVE THAT'S RICH IN PROBIOTICS, HEALTHY FATS, AND ANTIOXIDANTS. ENJOY!

CRISPY FRIED OYSTERS WITH TABASCO AIOLI

INGREDIENTS:
- 1 PINT FRESH SHUCKED OYSTERS, DRAINED
- 1 CUP ALL-PURPOSE FLOUR
- 1 TSP PAPRIKA
- 1/2 TSP GARLIC POWDER
- 1/2 TSP ONION POWDER
- 1/2 TSP SALT
- 1/4 TSP BLACK PEPPER
- 2 EGGS, BEATEN
- 2 TBSP MILK
- 2 CUPS PANKO BREADCRUMBS
- VEGETABLE OIL FOR FRYING
- FOR THE TABASCO AIOLI:
- 1/2 CUP MAYONNAISE
- 2 TBSP TABASCO SAUCE
- 1 TSP LEMON JUICE
- 1 GARLIC CLOVE, MINCED
- SALT AND PEPPER TO TASTE

INSTRUCTIONS:
1. RINSE THE OYSTERS AND PAT THEM DRY WITH PAPER TOWELS.
2. IN A SHALLOW DISH, COMBINE THE FLOUR, PAPRIKA, GARLIC POWDER, ONION POWDER, SALT, AND BLACK PEPPER.
3. IN A SEPARATE SHALLOW DISH, WHISK TOGETHER THE BEATEN EGGS AND MILK.
4. IN A THIRD SHALLOW DISH, PLACE THE PANKO BREADCRUMBS.
5. DREDGE THE OYSTERS IN THE FLOUR MIXTURE, SHAKING OFF ANY EXCESS. DIP THEM IN THE EGG MIXTURE, THEN COAT THEM IN THE PANKO BREADCRUMBS, PRESSING THE BREADCRUMBS ONTO THE OYSTERS TO ENSURE THEY ARE FULLY COATED.
6. HEAT ABOUT 1 INCH OF VEGETABLE OIL IN A LARGE SKILLET OVER MEDIUM-HIGH HEAT. WHEN THE OIL IS HOT, ADD THE OYSTERS IN BATCHES AND FRY UNTIL GOLDEN BROWN, TURNING ONCE, ABOUT 2-3 MINUTES PER SIDE. DRAIN THE FRIED OYSTERS ON PAPER TOWELS TO REMOVE ANY EXCESS OIL.
7. IN A SMALL BOWL, WHISK TOGETHER THE MAYONNAISE, TABASCO SAUCE, LEMON JUICE, MINCED GARLIC, SALT, AND PEPPER TO MAKE THE TABASCO AIOLI.
8. SERVE THE CRISPY FRIED OYSTERS HOT, WITH THE TABASCO AIOLI ON THE SIDE FOR DIPPING.

THIS RECIPE IS A DELICIOUS AND UNIQUE WAY TO ENJOY OYSTERS FOR LUNCH. THE CRISPY FRIED COATING PROVIDES A SATISFYING CRUNCH, WHILE THE SUCCULENT OYSTERS PROVIDE A BURST OF FLAVOUR WITH EVERY BITE. THE TABASCO AIOLI ADDS A SPICY AND TANGY KICK THAT PERFECTLY COMPLEMENTS THE OYSTERS. THIS RECIPE IS SURE TO IMPRESS ANYONE WHO LOVES SEAFOOD AND SPICY FLAVOURS!

BAKED SWEET POTATO WITH MISO TAHINI SAUCE

INGREDIENTS:
- 1 LARGE SWEET POTATO
- 1 TBSP OLIVE OIL
- 1 TBSP MISO PASTE
- 1 TBSP TAHINI
- 1 TSP HONEY
- 1 TSP RICE VINEGAR
- 1 GARLIC CLOVE, MINCED
- 2 TBSP WATER
- SALT AND PEPPER TO TASTE
- OPTIONAL TOPPINGS: SLICED GREEN ONIONS, SESAME SEEDS, CHOPPED CILANTRO

INSTRUCTIONS:
1. PREHEAT THE OVEN TO 400°F (200°C). LINE A BAKING SHEET WITH PARCHMENT PAPER.
2. SCRUB THE SWEET POTATO CLEAN AND PRICK IT A FEW TIMES WITH A FORK. RUB THE SKIN WITH OLIVE OIL AND PLACE IT ON THE PREPARED BAKING SHEET. BAKE FOR 40–50 MINUTES, OR UNTIL THE SWEET POTATO IS TENDER AND EASILY PIERCED WITH A FORK.
3. WHILE THE SWEET POTATO IS BAKING, PREPARE THE MISO TAHINI SAUCE. IN A SMALL BOWL, WHISK TOGETHER THE MISO PASTE, TAHINI, HONEY, RICE VINEGAR, GARLIC, AND WATER UNTIL SMOOTH. ADD MORE WATER IF NEEDED TO THIN THE SAUCE TO YOUR DESIRED CONSISTENCY.
4. WHEN THE SWEET POTATO IS DONE, REMOVE IT FROM THE OVEN AND CAREFULLY SLICE IT OPEN LENGTHWISE. USE A FORK TO MASH THE INSIDES A LITTLE BIT. DRIZZLE THE MISO TAHINI SAUCE OVER THE SWEET POTATO, AND SPRINKLE WITH SALT AND PEPPER TO TASTE.
5. TOP THE SWEET POTATO WITH SLICED GREEN ONIONS, SESAME SEEDS, AND CHOPPED CILANTRO IF DESIRED. SERVE HOT.

THIS DISH IS A UNIQUE AND HEALTHY WAY TO ENJOY A SWEET POTATO, AND THE MISO TAHINI SAUCE ADDS A SAVOURY UMAMI FLAVOUR THAT IS SURE TO IMPRESS. PLUS, THE SAUCE USES INGREDIENTS LIKE MISO PASTE AND TAHINI THAT AREN'T COMMONLY FOUND IN TRADITIONAL WESTERN CUISINE.

CHICKEN AVOCADO SALAD (DIFFERENT)

INGREDIENTS:
- 2 BONELESS, SKINLESS CHICKEN BREASTS
- SALT AND PEPPER TO TASTE
- 1 TBSP OLIVE OIL
- 4 CUPS MIXED GREENS
- 1 AVOCADO, DICED
- 1 CUP CHERRY TOMATOES, HALVED
- 1/4 CUP RED ONION, THINLY SLICED
- 1/4 CUP CRUMBLED FETA CHEESE
- 2 TBSP CHOPPED FRESH PARSLEY
- FOR THE DRESSING:
- 1/4 CUP OLIVE OIL
- 2 TBSP RED WINE VINEGAR
- 1 TSP HONEY
- 1 TSP DIJON MUSTARD
- 1 GARLIC CLOVE, MINCED
- SALT AND PEPPER TO TASTE

INSTRUCTIONS:
1. SEASON THE CHICKEN BREASTS WITH SALT AND PEPPER. HEAT THE OLIVE OIL IN A SKILLET OVER MEDIUM-HIGH HEAT. ADD THE CHICKEN BREASTS AND COOK FOR 5-6 MINUTES PER SIDE, OR UNTIL COOKED THROUGH. REMOVE FROM THE SKILLET AND LET COOL.
2. IN A LARGE BOWL, COMBINE THE MIXED GREENS, DICED AVOCADO, CHERRY TOMATOES, AND RED ONION.
3. IN A SMALL BOWL, WHISK TOGETHER THE OLIVE OIL, RED WINE VINEGAR, HONEY, DIJON MUSTARD, GARLIC, SALT, AND PEPPER TO MAKE THE DRESSING.
4. SLICE THE COOLED CHICKEN BREASTS INTO STRIPS AND ADD THEM TO THE SALAD. DRIZZLE THE DRESSING OVER THE SALAD AND TOSS TO COAT.
5. SPRINKLE THE CRUMBLED FETA CHEESE AND CHOPPED PARSLEY OVER THE TOP OF THE SALAD. SERVE IMMEDIATELY.

THIS SALAD IS DELICIOUS AND SATISFYING, AND THE COMBINATION OF JUICY CHERRY TOMATOES, CREAMY AVOCADO, AND TANGY FETA CHEESE CREATES A PERFECT BALANCE OF FLAVOURS. THE HOMEMADE DRESSING IS ALSO A TASTY ADDITION THAT YOU CAN EASILY MAKE WITH COMMON PANTRY INGREDIENTS.

RASPBERRY AND CHICKEN SALAD WITH BALSAMIC VINAIGRETTE

INGREDIENTS:
- 2 BONELESS, SKINLESS CHICKEN BREASTS
- SALT AND PEPPER TO TASTE
- 1 TBSP OLIVE OIL
- 6 CUPS MIXED GREENS
- 1 CUP FRESH RASPBERRIES
- 1/2 CUP CRUMBLED GOAT CHEESE
- 1/4 CUP SLICED ALMONDS
- FOR THE DRESSING:
- 1/4 CUP OLIVE OIL
- 2 TBSP BALSAMIC VINEGAR
- 1 TSP HONEY
- 1 TSP DIJON MUSTARD
- SALT AND PEPPER TO TASTE

INSTRUCTIONS:
1. SEASON THE CHICKEN BREASTS WITH SALT AND PEPPER. HEAT THE OLIVE OIL IN A SKILLET OVER MEDIUM-HIGH HEAT. ADD THE CHICKEN BREASTS AND COOK FOR 5-6 MINUTES PER SIDE, OR UNTIL COOKED THROUGH. REMOVE FROM THE SKILLET AND LET COOL.
2. IN A LARGE BOWL, COMBINE THE MIXED GREENS, FRESH RASPBERRIES, CRUMBLED GOAT CHEESE, AND SLICED ALMONDS.
3. IN A SMALL BOWL, WHISK TOGETHER THE OLIVE OIL, BALSAMIC VINEGAR, HONEY, DIJON MUSTARD, SALT, AND PEPPER TO MAKE THE DRESSING.
4. SLICE THE COOLED CHICKEN BREASTS INTO STRIPS AND ADD THEM TO THE SALAD. DRIZZLE THE DRESSING OVER THE SALAD AND TOSS TO COAT.
5. SERVE IMMEDIATELY.

THIS SALAD IS A REFRESHING AND FLAVOURFUL LUNCH DISH THAT IS PERFECT FOR SPRING AND SUMMER. THE JUICY RASPBERRIES ADD A SWEET AND TART FLAVOUR, WHILE THE CREAMY GOAT CHEESE AND CRUNCHY ALMONDS CREATE A NICE TEXTURE CONTRAST. THE BALSAMIC VINAIGRETTE TIES EVERYTHING TOGETHER WITH A TANGY AND SLIGHTLY SWEET TASTE.

QUINOA AND ROASTED VEGETABLE SALAD

INGREDIENTS:
- 1 CUP QUINOA, RINSED
- 2 CUPS WATER
- 1 MEDIUM SWEET POTATO, PEELED AND CUBED
- 1 RED BELL PEPPER, SEEDED AND DICED
- 1 ZUCCHINI, DICED
- 1/2 RED ONION, THINLY SLICED
- 2 TBSP OLIVE OIL
- SALT AND PEPPER TO TASTE
- 2 CUPS BABY SPINACH
- 1/4 CUP CRUMBLED FETA CHEESE
- FOR THE DRESSING:
- 1/4 CUP OLIVE OIL
- 2 TBSP LEMON JUICE
- 1 TSP HONEY
- 1 GARLIC CLOVE, MINCED
- SALT AND PEPPER TO TASTE

INSTRUCTIONS:
1. PREHEAT THE OVEN TO 400°F (200°C). LINE A BAKING SHEET WITH PARCHMENT PAPER.
2. IN A MEDIUM SAUCEPAN, COMBINE THE QUINOA AND WATER. BRING TO A BOIL, THEN REDUCE THE HEAT TO LOW AND SIMMER FOR 15–20 MINUTES, OR UNTIL THE QUINOA IS TENDER AND THE WATER IS ABSORBED. REMOVE FROM THE HEAT AND LET COOL.
3. IN A LARGE BOWL, TOSS THE SWEET POTATO, RED BELL PEPPER, ZUCCHINI, AND RED ONION WITH THE OLIVE OIL. SEASON WITH SALT AND PEPPER TO TASTE. SPREAD THE VEGETABLES OUT ON THE PREPARED BAKING SHEET AND ROAST FOR 20–25 MINUTES, OR UNTIL TENDER AND LIGHTLY BROWNED.
4. IN A SMALL BOWL, WHISK TOGETHER THE OLIVE OIL, LEMON JUICE, HONEY, GARLIC, SALT, AND PEPPER TO MAKE THE DRESSING.
5. IN A LARGE BOWL, COMBINE THE COOKED QUINOA, ROASTED VEGETABLES, AND BABY SPINACH. DRIZZLE THE DRESSING OVER THE TOP AND TOSS TO COAT.
6. SPRINKLE THE CRUMBLED FETA CHEESE OVER THE TOP OF THE SALAD. SERVE IMMEDIATELY.

THIS QUINOA AND ROASTED VEGETABLE SALAD IS A DELICIOUS AND HEALTHY LUNCH DISH THAT IS PACKED WITH NUTRIENTS AND FLAVOUR. THE ROASTED VEGETABLES ADD A DELICIOUS SWEETNESS AND A NICE CRUNCH TO THE DISH, WHILE THE FETA CHEESE ADDS A CREAMY TANGINESS. THE LEMONY DRESSING TIES EVERYTHING TOGETHER WITH A REFRESHING AND BRIGHT FLAVOUR.

BAKED SALMON AND ASPARAGUS WITH LEMON GARLIC BUTTER

INGREDIENTS:

- 4 SALMON FILLETS
- SALT AND PEPPER TO TASTE
- 1 LB ASPARAGUS, TRIMMED
- 2 TBSP OLIVE OIL
- FOR THE LEMON GARLIC BUTTER:
- 1/4 CUP BUTTER, SOFTENED
- 2 GARLIC CLOVES, MINCED
- ZEST OF 1 LEMON
- JUICE OF 1/2 LEMON
- SALT AND PEPPER TO TASTE

INSTRUCTIONS:
1. PREHEAT THE OVEN TO 400°F (200°C). LINE A BAKING SHEET WITH PARCHMENT PAPER.
2. SEASON THE SALMON FILLETS WITH SALT AND PEPPER. PLACE THEM ON THE PREPARED BAKING SHEET.
3. IN A SEPARATE BOWL, TOSS THE ASPARAGUS WITH THE OLIVE OIL. SEASON WITH SALT AND PEPPER TO TASTE. ARRANGE THE ASPARAGUS AROUND THE SALMON FILLETS ON THE BAKING SHEET.
4. BAKE FOR 12–15 MINUTES, OR UNTIL THE SALMON IS COOKED THROUGH AND THE ASPARAGUS IS TENDER.
5. IN A SMALL BOWL, MIX TOGETHER THE SOFTENED BUTTER, MINCED GARLIC, LEMON ZEST, LEMON JUICE, SALT, AND PEPPER TO MAKE THE LEMON GARLIC BUTTER.
6. REMOVE THE SALMON AND ASPARAGUS FROM THE OVEN. SPOON THE LEMON GARLIC BUTTER OVER THE TOP OF THE SALMON AND ASPARAGUS.
7. SERVE IMMEDIATELY.

THIS BAKED SALMON AND ASPARAGUS DISH IS A HEALTHY AND FLAVOURFUL LUNCH OPTION THAT IS EASY TO MAKE. THE TENDER ASPARAGUS COMPLEMENTS THE MOIST AND FLAKY SALMON PERFECTLY, AND THE LEMON GARLIC BUTTER ADDS A DELICIOUS TANGINESS AND A RICHNESS TO THE DISH. THIS RECIPE IS SURE TO IMPRESS YOUR TASTE BUDS AND ANYONE YOU SERVE IT TO!

ROASTED RADISH AND LENTIL SALAD

INGREDIENTS:
- 1 BUNCH OF RADISHES, TRIMMED AND SLICED
- 1 CUP OF GREEN LENTILS, RINSED AND DRAINED
- 2 CUPS OF WATER OR VEGETABLE BROTH
- 1/4 CUP OF CHOPPED WALNUTS
- 1/4 CUP OF CRUMBLED FETA CHEESE (OPTIONAL)
- 2 TABLESPOONS OF EXTRA-VIRGIN OLIVE OIL
- 1 TABLESPOON OF BALSAMIC VINEGAR
- 1 TEASPOON OF HONEY
- 1/4 TEASPOON OF SMOKED PAPRIKA
- SALT AND PEPPER TO TASTE

INSTRUCTIONS:
1. PREHEAT OVEN TO 400°F. TOSS SLICED RADISHES WITH A DRIZZLE OF OLIVE OIL, SMOKED PAPRIKA, SALT, AND PEPPER. SPREAD EVENLY ON A BAKING SHEET AND ROAST FOR 15-20 MINUTES OR UNTIL TENDER AND LIGHTLY BROWNED.
2. WHILE THE RADISHES ARE ROASTING, COMBINE THE RINSED LENTILS AND WATER OR VEGETABLE BROTH IN A MEDIUM-SIZED SAUCEPAN. BRING TO A BOIL, THEN REDUCE HEAT TO LOW AND COVER WITH A LID. COOK FOR 20-25 MINUTES OR UNTIL THE LENTILS ARE TENDER BUT NOT MUSHY. DRAIN ANY EXCESS LIQUID AND SET ASIDE.
3. IN A SMALL BOWL, WHISK TOGETHER THE OLIVE OIL, BALSAMIC VINEGAR, HONEY, AND A PINCH OF SALT UNTIL SMOOTH.
4. ASSEMBLE YOUR SALAD: IN A LARGE MIXING BOWL, COMBINE THE ROASTED RADISHES, COOKED LENTILS, CHOPPED WALNUTS, AND CRUMBLED FETA CHEESE (IF USING). DRIZZLE THE DRESSING OVER THE TOP AND TOSS TO COMBINE.
5. SERVE IMMEDIATELY AND ENJOY!

THIS SALAD IS A GREAT SOURCE OF PROTEIN, FIBRE, AND HEALTHY FATS, AND THE COMBINATION OF ROASTED RADISHES AND SMOKED PAPRIKA ADDS A DELICIOUS AND UNIQUE FLAVOUR TO THE DISH.

SPINACH AND CHICKPEA STEW

INGREDIENTS:
- 1 CAN OF CHICKPEAS, DRAINED AND RINSED
- 1 ONION, CHOPPED
- 2 CLOVES OF GARLIC, MINCED
- 2 CUPS OF VEGETABLE BROTH
- 1 CAN OF DICED TOMATOES
- 4 CUPS OF FRESH SPINACH LEAVES
- 1 TEASPOON OF GROUND CUMIN
- 1 TEASPOON OF GROUND CORIANDER
- 1/2 TEASPOON OF SMOKED PAPRIKA
- SALT AND PEPPER TO TASTE
- 1 TABLESPOON OF OLIVE OIL
- 1 LEMON, CUT INTO WEDGES

INSTRUCTIONS:
1. HEAT THE OLIVE OIL IN A LARGE POT OVER MEDIUM-HIGH HEAT. ADD THE CHOPPED ONION AND MINCED GARLIC AND SAUTÉ UNTIL THE ONION IS SOFT AND TRANSLUCENT, ABOUT 5 MINUTES.
2. ADD THE GROUND CUMIN, GROUND CORIANDER, AND SMOKED PAPRIKA TO THE POT AND STIR TO COMBINE. COOK FOR 1-2 MINUTES UNTIL FRAGRANT.
3. ADD THE DRAINED CHICKPEAS, VEGETABLE BROTH, AND DICED TOMATOES TO THE POT. BRING TO A BOIL, THEN REDUCE HEAT TO LOW AND SIMMER FOR 10-15 MINUTES OR UNTIL THE CHICKPEAS ARE TENDER AND THE STEW HAS THICKENED SLIGHTLY.
4. ADD THE FRESH SPINACH LEAVES TO THE POT AND STIR UNTIL WILTED, ABOUT 2-3 MINUTES.
5. SEASON THE STEW WITH SALT AND PEPPER TO TASTE.
6. SERVE THE SPINACH AND CHICKPEA STEW HOT WITH A WEDGE OF LEMON ON THE SIDE FOR SQUEEZING OVER THE TOP.

THIS HEARTY AND NUTRITIOUS STEW IS A GREAT SOURCE OF VITAMINS A, C, AND K, AS WELL AS PROTEIN, FIBRE, AND OTHER ESSENTIAL NUTRIENTS.

GRILLED CHICKEN AND VEGETABLE SKEWERS

INGREDIENTS:
- 1 LB. BONELESS, SKINLESS CHICKEN BREASTS, CUT INTO 1-INCH CUBES
- 2 BELL PEPPERS, CUT INTO 1-INCH PIECES
- 1 LARGE RED ONION, CUT INTO 1-INCH PIECES
- 1 ZUCCHINI, SLICED INTO ROUNDS
- 1 YELLOW SQUASH, SLICED INTO ROUNDS
- 2 TABLESPOONS OF OLIVE OIL
- 2 TABLESPOONS OF BALSAMIC VINEGAR
- 1 TABLESPOON OF DIJON MUSTARD
- 2 CLOVES OF GARLIC, MINCED
- SALT AND PEPPER TO TASTE
- WOODEN SKEWERS, SOAKED IN WATER FOR AT LEAST 30 MINUTES

INSTRUCTIONS:
1. PREHEAT GRILL OR GRILL PAN TO MEDIUM-HIGH HEAT.
2. IN A SMALL BOWL, WHISK TOGETHER THE OLIVE OIL, BALSAMIC VINEGAR, DIJON MUSTARD, MINCED GARLIC, SALT, AND PEPPER.
3. THREAD THE CHICKEN CUBES, BELL PEPPER PIECES, RED ONION PIECES, ZUCCHINI ROUNDS, AND YELLOW SQUASH ROUNDS ONTO THE WOODEN SKEWERS.
4. BRUSH THE SKEWERS WITH THE MARINADE, MAKING SURE TO COAT ALL SIDES.
5. GRILL THE SKEWERS FOR 10-12 MINUTES, TURNING OCCASIONALLY, OR UNTIL THE CHICKEN IS COOKED THROUGH AND THE VEGETABLES ARE TENDER AND SLIGHTLY CHARRED.
6. SERVE THE GRILLED CHICKEN AND VEGETABLE SKEWERS HOT, GARNISHED WITH FRESH HERBS IF DESIRED.

THIS DISH IS HIGH IN PROTEIN FROM THE CHICKEN AND LOW IN FAT THANKS TO THE USE OF LEAN CHICKEN BREAST AND HEALTHY FATS FROM THE OLIVE OIL. THE GRILLED VEGETABLES ALSO PROVIDE A GOOD SOURCE OF VITAMINS AND MINERALS.

DUCK AND HADDOCK CHOWDER

INGREDIENTS:
- 1/2 LB. DUCK BREAST, SKIN REMOVED AND DICED
- 1/2 LB. HADDOCK FILLET, DICED
- 4 SLICES OF BACON, DICED
- 1 LARGE ONION, DICED
- 2 CLOVES OF GARLIC, MINCED
- 2 CUPS OF CHICKEN OR VEGETABLE BROTH
- 1 CUP OF HEAVY CREAM
- 2 CUPS OF DICED POTATOES
- 1 CUP OF FROZEN CORN KERNELS
- 1 TEASPOON OF DRIED THYME
- SALT AND PEPPER TO TASTE

INSTRUCTIONS:
1. IN A LARGE POT OR DUTCH OVEN, COOK THE DICED BACON OVER MEDIUM HEAT UNTIL CRISPY. REMOVE THE BACON WITH A SLOTTED SPOON AND SET ASIDE.
2. ADD THE DICED DUCK BREAST TO THE POT AND COOK UNTIL BROWNED AND CRISPY, ABOUT 5-7 MINUTES. REMOVE THE DUCK WITH A SLOTTED SPOON AND SET ASIDE.
3. ADD THE DICED ONION TO THE POT AND SAUTÉ UNTIL SOFT AND TRANSLUCENT, ABOUT 5 MINUTES. ADD THE MINCED GARLIC AND SAUTÉ FOR ANOTHER MINUTE.
4. ADD THE CHICKEN OR VEGETABLE BROTH, DICED POTATOES, AND DRIED THYME TO THE POT. BRING TO A BOIL, THEN REDUCE HEAT TO LOW AND SIMMER FOR 10-15 MINUTES OR UNTIL THE POTATOES ARE TENDER.
5. ADD THE DICED HADDOCK AND FROZEN CORN KERNELS TO THE POT AND SIMMER FOR ANOTHER 5-7 MINUTES OR UNTIL THE HADDOCK IS COOKED THROUGH.
6. STIR IN THE HEAVY CREAM AND RESERVED BACON AND DUCK. SEASON THE CHOWDER WITH SALT AND PEPPER TO TASTE.
7. SERVE THE DUCK AND HADDOCK CHOWDER HOT, GARNISHED WITH FRESH HERBS IF DESIRED.

THIS HEARTY AND FLAVOURFUL CHOWDER IS A GREAT WAY TO COMBINE TWO UNIQUE PROTEINS - DUCK AND HADDOCK - IN A DELICIOUS AND SATISFYING MEAL.

ORANGE AND AVOCADO SALAD WITH QUINOA

INGREDIENTS:
- 1 CUP OF QUINOA, RINSED
- 2 CUPS OF WATER
- 2 ORANGES, PEELED AND SLICED
- 1 AVOCADO, PEELED AND SLICED
- 1/2 RED ONION, THINLY SLICED
- 1/2 CUP OF CRUMBLED FETA CHEESE
- 1/4 CUP OF CHOPPED FRESH CILANTRO
- 2 TABLESPOONS OF OLIVE OIL
- 2 TABLESPOONS OF RED WINE VINEGAR
- SALT AND PEPPER TO TASTE

INSTRUCTIONS:
1. IN A MEDIUM POT, BRING THE QUINOA AND WATER TO A BOIL. REDUCE HEAT TO LOW, COVER, AND SIMMER FOR 15-20 MINUTES OR UNTIL THE QUINOA IS TENDER AND THE WATER HAS BEEN ABSORBED.
2. IN A LARGE BOWL, WHISK TOGETHER THE OLIVE OIL, RED WINE VINEGAR, SALT, AND PEPPER.
3. ADD THE COOKED QUINOA TO THE BOWL AND TOSS TO COAT IN THE DRESSING.
4. ADD THE SLICED ORANGES, SLICED AVOCADO, AND THINLY SLICED RED ONION TO THE BOWL AND GENTLY TOSS TO COMBINE.
5. SPRINKLE THE CRUMBLED FETA CHEESE AND CHOPPED CILANTRO OVER THE TOP OF THE SALAD.
6. SERVE THE ORANGE AND AVOCADO SALAD WITH QUINOA IMMEDIATELY, GARNISHED WITH ADDITIONAL CILANTRO IF DESIRED.

THIS VIBRANT AND FLAVOURFUL SALAD IS A GREAT SOURCE OF FIBRE, HEALTHY FATS, AND ESSENTIAL VITAMINS AND MINERALS. THE ADDITION OF ORANGES ADDS A BURST OF CITRUSY SWEETNESS, WHILE THE CREAMY AVOCADO AND TANGY FETA CHEESE PROVIDE A SATISFYING TEXTURE AND FLAVOUR CONTRAST.

MANGO AND BLACK BEAN SALAD WITH CASHEW DRESSING

INGREDIENTS:
- 1 CAN OF BLACK BEANS, DRAINED AND RINSED
- 1 RIPE MANGO, PEELED AND DICED
- 1 SMALL RED ONION, DICED
- 1/4 CUP OF CHOPPED FRESH CILANTRO
- 2 TABLESPOONS OF LIME JUICE
- 1 TABLESPOON OF HONEY
- 1/4 CUP OF ROASTED CASHEWS
- 1/4 CUP OF WATER
- 1 SMALL GARLIC CLOVE, MINCED
- 1/2 TEASPOON OF GROUND CUMIN
- SALT AND PEPPER TO TASTE

INSTRUCTIONS:
1. IN A LARGE BOWL, COMBINE THE BLACK BEANS, DICED MANGO, DICED RED ONION, AND CHOPPED CILANTRO.
2. IN A BLENDER OR FOOD PROCESSOR, COMBINE THE ROASTED CASHEWS, WATER, GARLIC CLOVE, GROUND CUMIN, LIME JUICE, HONEY, AND A PINCH OF SALT AND PEPPER. BLEND UNTIL SMOOTH AND CREAMY, ADDING MORE WATER IF NECESSARY TO THIN OUT THE DRESSING.
3. POUR THE CASHEW DRESSING OVER THE BLACK BEAN AND MANGO MIXTURE AND TOSS TO COAT.
4. SERVE THE MANGO AND BLACK BEAN SALAD COLD, GARNISHED WITH ADDITIONAL CILANTRO IF DESIRED.

THIS SALAD IS A UNIQUE AND FLAVOURFUL COMBINATION OF SWEET AND SAVOURY INGREDIENTS, WITH THE ADDED CRUNCH OF ROASTED CASHEWS AND A CREAMY CASHEW DRESSING. THE BLACK BEANS PROVIDE A GOOD SOURCE OF PROTEIN AND FIBRE, WHILE THE MANGO ADDS A TROPICAL SWEETNESS TO THE DISH.

KIWI AND BANANA SMOOTHIE BOWL

INGREDIENTS:

·2 RIPE BANANAS, PEELED AND SLICED
·2 KIWIS, PEELED AND SLICED
·1 CUP OF FROZEN MANGO CHUNKS
·1/2 CUP OF COCONUT MILK
·1 TABLESPOON OF HONEY
·1 TABLESPOON OF CHIA SEEDS
·1/4 CUP OF GRANOLA
·FRESH MINT LEAVES FOR GARNISH (OPTIONAL)

INSTRUCTIONS:

1. IN A BLENDER, COMBINE THE SLICED BANANAS, SLICED KIWIS, FROZEN MANGO CHUNKS, COCONUT MILK, HONEY, AND CHIA SEEDS. BLEND UNTIL SMOOTH AND CREAMY.
2. POUR THE SMOOTHIE INTO A BOWL AND TOP WITH THE GRANOLA.
3. GARNISH THE SMOOTHIE BOWL WITH FRESH MINT LEAVES, IF DESIRED.
4. SERVE THE KIWI AND BANANA SMOOTHIE BOWL IMMEDIATELY, ENJOYING THE REFRESHING AND FRUITY FLAVOURS.

THIS SMOOTHIE BOWL IS A GREAT WAY TO ENJOY THE NATURAL SWEETNESS OF KIWIS AND BANANAS WHILE GETTING A BOOST OF HEALTHY NUTRIENTS FROM THE CHIA SEEDS AND GRANOLA. THE COCONUT MILK ADDS A CREAMY AND TROPICAL TWIST TO THE SMOOTHIE, MAKING IT A SATISFYING AND FILLING LUNCH DISH.

GRILLED CHICKEN AND SWEET POTATO BOWL

INGREDIENTS:
- 1 MEDIUM SWEET POTATO, PEELED AND DICED
- 2 CHICKEN BREASTS
- 2 TABLESPOONS OF OLIVE OIL
- 2 TEASPOONS OF SMOKED PAPRIKA
- 1 TEASPOON OF GARLIC POWDER
- 1/2 TEASPOON OF GROUND CUMIN
- SALT AND PEPPER TO TASTE
- 1 AVOCADO, PEELED AND SLICED
- 1/2 CUP OF CHERRY TOMATOES, HALVED
- 1/4 CUP OF CRUMBLED FETA CHEESE
- FRESH PARSLEY OR CILANTRO FOR GARNISH (OPTIONAL)

INSTRUCTIONS:
1. PREHEAT THE GRILL OR GRILL PAN TO MEDIUM-HIGH HEAT.
2. IN A BOWL, TOSS THE DICED SWEET POTATO WITH 1 TABLESPOON OF OLIVE OIL, SMOKED PAPRIKA, GARLIC POWDER, CUMIN, SALT, AND PEPPER.
3. GRILL THE CHICKEN BREASTS FOR 6-7 MINUTES PER SIDE OR UNTIL COOKED THROUGH.
4. GRILL THE SWEET POTATO CUBES FOR 8-10 MINUTES OR UNTIL TENDER AND LIGHTLY CHARRED.
5. IN A LARGE BOWL, COMBINE THE GRILLED SWEET POTATO CUBES, SLICED AVOCADO, HALVED CHERRY TOMATOES, AND CRUMBLED FETA CHEESE.
6. SLICE THE GRILLED CHICKEN BREASTS AND ADD THEM TO THE BOWL.
7. DRIZZLE THE REMAINING TABLESPOON OF OLIVE OIL OVER THE TOP OF THE BOWL AND TOSS TO COMBINE.
8. SERVE THE GRILLED CHICKEN AND SWEET POTATO BOWL IMMEDIATELY, GARNISHED WITH FRESH PARSLEY OR CILANTRO IF DESIRED.

THIS LUNCH DISH IS A GREAT SOURCE OF LEAN PROTEIN, COMPLEX CARBOHYDRATES, HEALTHY FATS, AND ESSENTIAL VITAMINS AND MINERALS. THE GRILLED CHICKEN PROVIDES A GOOD AMOUNT OF PROTEIN, WHILE THE SWEET POTATOES OFFER A HEALTHY SOURCE OF CARBOHYDRATES AND FIBRE. THE AVOCADO ADDS A DOSE OF HEALTHY FATS, WHILE THE FETA CHEESE AND CHERRY TOMATOES PROVIDE A SATISFYING BURST OF FLAVOUR.

CELERY AND COCKLES SALAD WITH ALMOND VINAIGRETTE

INGREDIENTS:
- 2 CUPS OF COOKED COCKLES, DRAINED AND RINSED
- 2 CUPS OF CHOPPED CELERY
- 1/4 CUP OF SLICED ALMONDS
- 1 TABLESPOON OF DIJON MUSTARD
- 1 TABLESPOON OF HONEY
- 1/4 CUP OF WHITE WINE VINEGAR
- 1/2 CUP OF OLIVE OIL
- SALT AND PEPPER TO TASTE
- FRESH PARSLEY OR CILANTRO FOR GARNISH (OPTIONAL)

INSTRUCTIONS:
1. IN A LARGE BOWL, COMBINE THE COOKED COCKLES AND CHOPPED CELERY.
2. IN A SMALL BOWL, WHISK TOGETHER THE DIJON MUSTARD, HONEY, WHITE WINE VINEGAR, OLIVE OIL, AND A PINCH OF SALT AND PEPPER TO MAKE THE ALMOND VINAIGRETTE.
3. POUR THE ALMOND VINAIGRETTE OVER THE COCKLES AND CELERY AND TOSS TO COAT.
4. SPRINKLE THE SLICED ALMONDS OVER THE TOP OF THE SALAD.
5. GARNISH THE SALAD WITH FRESH PARSLEY OR CILANTRO, IF DESIRED.
6. SERVE THE CELERY AND COCKLES SALAD IMMEDIATELY, ENJOYING THE UNIQUE COMBINATION OF FLAVOURS AND TEXTURES.

THIS SALAD IS A GREAT WAY TO ENJOY THE UNIQUE FLAVOUR OF COCKLES, WHICH ARE A TYPE OF SMALL SHELLFISH THAT ARE RICH IN PROTEIN AND ESSENTIAL NUTRIENTS. THE CELERY ADDS A SATISFYING CRUNCH TO THE SALAD, WHILE THE SLICED ALMONDS PROVIDE A NUTTY AND CRUNCHY TEXTURE. THE ALMOND VINAIGRETTE TIES ALL OF THE FLAVOURS TOGETHER, CREATING A DELICIOUS AND HEALTHY LUNCH DISH.

LEMONY ROASTED CAULIFLOWER WITH ROASTED VEGETABLES AND A FRESH HERB DRESSING

INGREDIENTS:
- 1 LARGE HEAD CAULIFLOWER, CUT INTO FLORETS
- 2 LEMONS, SLICED
- 2 LARGE CARROTS, PEELED AND SLICED
- 1 LARGE RED ONION, SLICED
- 1 LARGE SWEET POTATO, PEELED AND DICED
- 2 TBSP OLIVE OIL
- SALT AND PEPPER TO TASTE

FOR THE DRESSING:
- 1/2 CUP CHOPPED FRESH PARSLEY
- 1/2 CUP CHOPPED FRESH MINT
- 1/4 CUP OLIVE OIL
- 2 TBSP LEMON JUICE
- 1 GARLIC CLOVE, MINCED
- SALT AND PEPPER TO TASTE

INSTRUCTIONS:
1. PREHEAT THE OVEN TO 425°F (220°C).
2. IN A LARGE BOWL, TOSS THE CAULIFLOWER, CARROTS, RED ONION, AND SWEET POTATO WITH OLIVE OIL, SALT, AND PEPPER UNTIL EVENLY COATED. SPREAD THE VEGETABLES OUT IN A SINGLE LAYER ON A LARGE BAKING SHEET.
3. ARRANGE THE LEMON SLICES ON TOP OF THE VEGETABLES.
4. ROAST THE VEGETABLES IN THE PREHEATED OVEN FOR 20-25 MINUTES, OR UNTIL TENDER AND LIGHTLY BROWNED.
5. WHILE THE VEGETABLES ARE ROASTING, PREPARE THE DRESSING BY WHISKING TOGETHER THE PARSLEY, MINT, OLIVE OIL, LEMON JUICE, GARLIC, SALT, AND PEPPER IN A SMALL BOWL.
6. ONCE THE VEGETABLES ARE DONE ROASTING, TRANSFER THEM TO A LARGE BOWL AND TOSS WITH THE FRESH HERB DRESSING. SERVE WARM OR AT ROOM TEMPERATURE.

LEMONY PRAWN STIR-FRY

INGREDIENTS:
- 1 LB (500G) LARGE PRAWNS, PEELED AND DEVEINED
- 2 GARLIC CLOVES, MINCED
- 1 INCH (2.5CM) PIECE OF GINGER, PEELED AND GRATED
- 1 RED BELL PEPPER, SLICED
- 1 YELLOW BELL PEPPER, SLICED
- 1 SMALL ONION, SLICED
- 1 SMALL ZUCCHINI, SLICED
- 1 SMALL CARROT, PEELED AND SLICED
- 2 TBSP OLIVE OIL
- SALT AND PEPPER TO TASTE
- 2 TBSP CHOPPED FRESH CILANTRO OR PARSLEY, FOR GARNISH

FOR THE SAUCE:
- 1/4 CUP (60ML) SOY SAUCE
- 2 TBSP LEMON JUICE
- 1 TBSP HONEY
- 1 TSP CORN-STARCH
- 1 TSP SESAME OIL

INSTRUCTIONS:
1. IN A SMALL BOWL, WHISK TOGETHER THE SOY SAUCE, LEMON JUICE, HONEY, CORN-STARCH, AND SESAME OIL UNTIL SMOOTH. SET ASIDE.
2. HEAT THE OLIVE OIL IN A LARGE SKILLET OR WOK OVER HIGH HEAT.
3. ADD THE GARLIC AND GINGER AND STIR-FRY FOR 30 SECONDS, OR UNTIL FRAGRANT.
4. ADD THE PRAWNS AND STIR-FRY FOR 2-3 MINUTES, OR UNTIL THEY TURN PINK AND ARE COOKED THROUGH.
5. ADD THE SLICED BELL PEPPERS, ONION, ZUCCHINI, AND CARROT AND STIR-FRY FOR ANOTHER 2-3 MINUTES, OR UNTIL THE VEGETABLES ARE TENDER-CRISP.
6. POUR THE SAUCE OVER THE PRAWN AND VEGETABLE MIXTURE AND STIR-FRY FOR ANOTHER MINUTE, OR UNTIL THE SAUCE THICKENS AND COATS EVERYTHING EVENLY.
7. REMOVE FROM THE HEAT AND SPRINKLE WITH CHOPPED CILANTRO OR PARSLEY. SERVE OVER STEAMED RICE OR QUINOA, IF DESIRED. ENJOY!

TASTY CHICKEN WRAPS WITH CUCUMBER AND AVOCADO

INGREDIENTS:
- 2 BONELESS, SKINLESS CHICKEN BREASTS
- 1/2 TSP CUMIN
- 1/2 TSP CHILI POWDER
- SALT AND PEPPER TO TASTE
- 2 TBSP OLIVE OIL
- 4 WHOLE WHEAT OR WHOLE GRAIN TORTILLAS OR WRAPS
- 1 SMALL CUCUMBER, SLICED
- 1 AVOCADO, SLICED
- 1/4 CUP PLAIN GREEK YOGURT
- 1 GARLIC CLOVE, MINCED
- 2 TBSP CHOPPED FRESH CILANTRO OR PARSLEY
- JUICE OF 1/2 LIME

INSTRUCTIONS:
1. PREHEAT THE OVEN TO 400°F (200°C).
2. SEASON THE CHICKEN BREASTS WITH CUMIN, CHILI POWDER, SALT, AND PEPPER.
3. HEAT THE OLIVE OIL IN A LARGE SKILLET OVER MEDIUM-HIGH HEAT. ADD THE CHICKEN BREASTS AND COOK FOR 4-5 MINUTES PER SIDE, OR UNTIL GOLDEN BROWN AND COOKED THROUGH.
4. TRANSFER THE CHICKEN TO A BAKING SHEET AND ROAST IN THE PREHEATED OVEN FOR 10-12 MINUTES, OR UNTIL FULLY COOKED. LET COOL FOR A FEW MINUTES, THEN SLICE INTO STRIPS.
5. IN A SMALL BOWL, WHISK TOGETHER THE GREEK YOGURT, GARLIC, CILANTRO OR PARSLEY, AND LIME JUICE.
6. LAY OUT THE TORTILLAS OR WRAPS AND SPREAD A DOLLOP OF THE YOGURT SAUCE ON EACH ONE.
7. TOP WITH SLICED CUCUMBER, AVOCADO, AND CHICKEN STRIPS.
8. FOLD THE BOTTOM OF THE WRAP UP OVER THE FILLING, THEN FOLD IN THE SIDES AND ROLL UP TIGHTLY.
9. SERVE IMMEDIATELY, OR WRAP IN PLASTIC WRAP AND REFRIGERATE UNTIL READY TO EAT.

ENJOY THE HEALTH BENEFITS OF THE AVOCADO, CUCUMBER, AND WHOLE GRAINS, AND SAVOUR THE DELICIOUS FLAVOURS OF THE SPICES AND CREAMY YOGURT SAUCE!

GARLIC, CHILI AND MINT SOUP

INGREDIENTS:
- 6 CUPS VEGETABLE BROTH
- 1 HEAD OF GARLIC, PEELED AND MINCED
- 1 RED CHILI PEPPER, SEEDED AND CHOPPED
- 2 TBSP OLIVE OIL
- 1 CAN (15 OZ/ 400G) CHICKPEAS, DRAINED AND RINSED
- 1 CUP CHOPPED FRESH MINT LEAVES
- JUICE OF 1 LEMON
- SALT AND PEPPER TO TASTE

INSTRUCTIONS:
1. IN A LARGE POT, HEAT THE OLIVE OIL OVER MEDIUM HEAT.
2. ADD THE MINCED GARLIC AND CHOPPED CHILI PEPPER AND SAUTÉ FOR 1-2 MINUTES, OR UNTIL FRAGRANT.
3. ADD THE VEGETABLE BROTH AND CHICKPEAS AND BRING TO A SIMMER.
4. LET THE SOUP SIMMER FOR 10-15 MINUTES, OR UNTIL THE FLAVOURS HAVE MELDED TOGETHER AND THE CHICKPEAS ARE TENDER.
5. STIR IN THE CHOPPED MINT LEAVES AND LEMON JUICE.
6. SEASON WITH SALT AND PEPPER TO TASTE.
7. SERVE HOT, GARNISHED WITH ADDITIONAL MINT LEAVES IF DESIRED.

THIS SOUP IS A GREAT SOURCE OF FIBRE, PROTEIN, AND VITAMIN C FROM THE CHICKPEAS, AND THE GARLIC AND CHILI ADD IMMUNE-BOOSTING PROPERTIES. THE FRESH MINT LEAVES PROVIDE A BURST OF FLAVOUR AND A REFRESHING AROMA. ENJOY!

CRAB AND BEETROOT SALAD

INGREDIENTS:
- 1 LB FRESH CRABMEAT
- 2 MEDIUM BEETROOTS, COOKED AND SLICED
- 1/2 SMALL RED ONION, THINLY SLICED
- 1 AVOCADO, SLICED
- 2 TBSP CHOPPED FRESH PARSLEY
- 1 TBSP CHOPPED FRESH MINT
- 1 TBSP LEMON JUICE
- 2 TBSP OLIVE OIL
- SALT AND PEPPER TO TASTE

INSTRUCTIONS:
1. IN A LARGE BOWL, MIX THE CRABMEAT, SLICED BEETROOT, AND RED ONION.
2. ADD THE SLICED AVOCADO, PARSLEY, AND MINT.
3. IN A SMALL BOWL, WHISK TOGETHER THE LEMON JUICE, OLIVE OIL, SALT, AND PEPPER.
4. POUR THE DRESSING OVER THE SALAD AND TOSS GENTLY TO COMBINE.
5. DIVIDE THE SALAD BETWEEN FOUR PLATES AND SERVE IMMEDIATELY.

THIS SALAD IS PACKED WITH PROTEIN FROM THE CRABMEAT, AND THE BEETROOT ADDS A HEALTHY DOSE OF VITAMINS AND MINERALS. THE AVOCADO ADDS HEALTHY FATS, WHILE THE FRESH HERBS AND LEMON JUICE GIVE THE SALAD A BRIGHT AND REFRESHING FLAVOUR. ENJOY!

RAINBOW FRUIT AND VEGETABLE SALAD

INGREDIENTS:
- 1 MEDIUM RED BELL PEPPER, SLICED
- 1 MEDIUM YELLOW BELL PEPPER, SLICED
- 1 MEDIUM ORANGE BELL PEPPER, SLICED
- 2 MEDIUM CARROTS, PEELED AND JULIENNED
- 1 MEDIUM BEETROOT, PEELED AND JULIENNED
- 1 MEDIUM CUCUMBER, SLICED
- 1 MEDIUM MANGO, PEELED AND CUBED
- 1 MEDIUM AVOCADO, CUBED
- 2 TBSP CHOPPED FRESH CILANTRO
- JUICE OF 1 LIME
- 1 TBSP HONEY
- SALT AND PEPPER TO TASTE

INSTRUCTIONS:
1. IN A LARGE BOWL, MIX TOGETHER THE SLICED BELL PEPPERS, JULIENNED CARROTS AND BEETROOT, AND SLICED CUCUMBER.
2. ADD THE CUBED MANGO AND AVOCADO.
3. IN A SMALL BOWL, WHISK TOGETHER THE LIME JUICE, HONEY, SALT, AND PEPPER.
4. POUR THE DRESSING OVER THE SALAD AND TOSS GENTLY TO COMBINE.
5. GARNISH WITH FRESH CILANTRO AND SERVE IMMEDIATELY.

THIS COLOURFUL SALAD IS PACKED WITH VITAMINS, MINERALS, AND FIBRE FROM THE VARIETY OF FRUITS AND VEGETABLES. THE DRESSING IS SWEET AND TANGY, AND THE FRESH CILANTRO ADDS A POP OF FLAVOUR. ENJOY AS A LIGHT AND HEALTHY MEAL OR AS A SIDE DISH.

VEGETABLE PIE

INGREDIENTS:
- 2 CUPS COOKED AND MASHED SWEET POTATO
- 2 CUPS COOKED AND MASHED BUTTERNUT SQUASH
- 1 SMALL HEAD OF BROCCOLI, CHOPPED
- 1 SMALL RED ONION, DICED
- 1 SMALL RED BELL PEPPER, DICED
- 2 CLOVES OF GARLIC, MINCED
- 1 TBSP OLIVE OIL
- 1 TSP DRIED THYME
- SALT AND PEPPER TO TASTE
- 1 SHEET OF PUFF PASTRY, THAWED
- 1 EGG, BEATEN

INSTRUCTIONS:
1. PREHEAT THE OVEN TO 375°F (190°C).
2. IN A LARGE BOWL, MIX TOGETHER THE MASHED SWEET POTATO AND BUTTERNUT SQUASH.
3. IN A SKILLET, SAUTÉ THE BROCCOLI, RED ONION, RED BELL PEPPER, AND GARLIC IN OLIVE OIL UNTIL THE VEGETABLES ARE TENDER.
4. ADD THE SAUTÉED VEGETABLES TO THE SWEET POTATO AND BUTTERNUT SQUASH MIXTURE. SEASON WITH THYME, SALT, AND PEPPER.
5. ROLL OUT THE PUFF PASTRY SHEET AND PLACE IT IN A GREASED 9-INCH PIE DISH.
6. POUR THE VEGETABLE MIXTURE INTO THE PIE DISH.
7. BRUSH THE EDGES OF THE PUFF PASTRY WITH BEATEN EGG.
8. BAKE IN THE PREHEATED OVEN FOR 25-30 MINUTES, OR UNTIL THE PASTRY IS GOLDEN BROWN.
9. SERVE HOT AND ENJOY!

THIS VEGETABLE PIE IS PACKED WITH NUTRIENTS FROM THE VARIETY OF VEGETABLES, AND THE SWEET POTATO AND BUTTERNUT SQUASH PROVIDE A HEALTHY DOSE OF FIBRE AND VITAMINS. THE PUFF PASTRY ADDS A FLAKY CRUST WITHOUT THE ADDED CALORIES OF A TRADITIONAL PIE CRUST. ENJOY AS A HEALTHY AND SATISFYING MEAL.

BAKED SWEET POTATO CHIPS WITH DUCK

INGREDIENTS:
- 2 MEDIUM SWEET POTATOES, PEELED AND THINLY SLICED
- 2 TBSP OLIVE OIL
- 1 TSP SMOKED PAPRIKA
- SALT AND PEPPER TO TASTE
- 2 DUCK BREASTS
- 1 TBSP HONEY
- 1 TBSP SOY SAUCE
- 1 TSP GRATED FRESH GINGER
- 1 CLOVE GARLIC, MINCED
- 1 TSP SESAME OIL

INSTRUCTIONS:
1. PREHEAT THE OVEN TO 400°F (200°C).
2. IN A LARGE BOWL, TOSS THE SWEET POTATO SLICES WITH OLIVE OIL, SMOKED PAPRIKA, SALT, AND PEPPER UNTIL COATED.
3. SPREAD THE SWEET POTATO SLICES IN A SINGLE LAYER ON A BAKING SHEET LINED WITH PARCHMENT PAPER.
4. BAKE IN THE PREHEATED OVEN FOR 15-20 MINUTES, OR UNTIL THE SWEET POTATO CHIPS ARE CRISPY AND GOLDEN BROWN.
5. WHILE THE SWEET POTATO CHIPS ARE BAKING, SCORE THE SKIN OF THE DUCK BREASTS WITH A SHARP KNIFE AND SEASON WITH SALT AND PEPPER.
6. HEAT A SKILLET OVER MEDIUM-HIGH HEAT AND PLACE THE DUCK BREASTS, SKIN SIDE DOWN, IN THE SKILLET.
7. COOK FOR 6-7 MINUTES, OR UNTIL THE SKIN IS CRISPY AND GOLDEN BROWN.
8. IN A SMALL BOWL, WHISK TOGETHER THE HONEY, SOY SAUCE, GRATED GINGER, MINCED GARLIC, AND SESAME OIL.
9. FLIP THE DUCK BREASTS OVER AND BRUSH WITH THE HONEY SOY GLAZE.
10. TRANSFER THE SKILLET TO THE PREHEATED OVEN AND BAKE FOR 8-10 MINUTES, OR UNTIL THE DUCK BREASTS ARE COOKED TO YOUR DESIRED LEVEL OF DONENESS.
11. SLICE THE DUCK BREASTS AND SERVE WITH THE BAKED SWEET POTATO CHIPS.

THIS DISH IS A HEALTHIER TAKE ON TRADITIONAL CHIPS AND DUCK, USING SWEET POTATO CHIPS INSTEAD OF DEEP-FRIED POTATOES AND COOKING THE DUCK BREASTS IN THE OVEN RATHER THAN PAN-FRYING. THE HONEY SOY GLAZE ADDS A SWEET AND SAVOURY FLAVOUR TO THE DISH, WHILE THE SWEET POTATO CHIPS PROVIDE A CRUNCHY TEXTURE. ENJOY!

HEALTHY STIR-FRY RECIPE:

INGREDIENTS:
- 1 LB CHICKEN BREAST, SLICED
- 2 TBSP CORN-STARCH
- 2 TBSP VEGETABLE OIL
- 1 RED BELL PEPPER, SLICED
- 1 YELLOW BELL PEPPER, SLICED
- 1 SMALL ONION, SLICED
- 2 CLOVES GARLIC, MINCED
- 1 TBSP GRATED FRESH GINGER
- 1 CUP SNOW PEAS
- 2 TBSP LOW-SODIUM SOY SAUCE
- 2 TBSP HOISIN SAUCE
- 1 TSP HONEY
- 1 TSP SESAME OIL
- SALT AND PEPPER TO TASTE
- CHOPPED GREEN ONIONS AND SESAME SEEDS FOR GARNISH

INSTRUCTIONS:
1. IN A LARGE BOWL, TOSS THE SLICED CHICKEN BREAST WITH CORN-STARCH UNTIL COATED.
2. HEAT A WOK OR LARGE SKILLET OVER HIGH HEAT AND ADD 1 TBSP OF VEGETABLE OIL.
3. ADD THE CHICKEN TO THE WOK AND STIR-FRY FOR 3-4 MINUTES, OR UNTIL BROWNED AND COOKED THROUGH.
4. REMOVE THE CHICKEN FROM THE WOK AND SET ASIDE.
5. ADD ANOTHER TABLESPOON OF VEGETABLE OIL TO THE WOK AND STIR-FRY THE RED AND YELLOW BELL PEPPERS, ONION, GARLIC, AND GINGER FOR 2-3 MINUTES, OR UNTIL THE VEGETABLES ARE TENDER.
6. ADD THE SNOW PEAS TO THE WOK AND STIR-FRY FOR ANOTHER MINUTE.
7. IN A SMALL BOWL, WHISK TOGETHER THE LOW-SODIUM SOY SAUCE, HOISIN SAUCE, HONEY, SESAME OIL, SALT, AND PEPPER.
8. ADD THE COOKED CHICKEN BACK TO THE WOK AND POUR THE SAUCE OVER THE CHICKEN AND VEGETABLES.
9. STIR-FRY FOR ANOTHER MINUTE, OR UNTIL THE SAUCE IS EVENLY DISTRIBUTED AND EVERYTHING IS HEATED THROUGH.
10. SERVE HOT AND GARNISH WITH CHOPPED GREEN ONIONS AND SESAME SEEDS.

THIS STIR-FRY IS PACKED WITH FLAVOUR FROM THE COMBINATION OF VEGETABLES AND SAVOURY SAUCE. USING CORN-STARCH INSTEAD OF FLOUR TO COAT THE CHICKEN HELPS TO REDUCE THE AMOUNT OF CARBS IN THE DISH, WHILE THE SNOW PEAS AND BELL PEPPERS PROVIDE A HEALTHY DOSE OF VITAMINS AND FIBRE. ENJOY THIS HEALTHY AND DELICIOUS STIR-FRY AS A SATISFYING MEAL.

MEXICAN-STYLE QUINOA STUFFED BELL PEPPERS WITH CORN AND BLACK BEANS

INGREDIENTS:

- 4 LARGE BELL PEPPERS (ANY COLOUR)
- 1 CUP QUINOA, RINSED
- 1 CAN BLACK BEANS, DRAINED AND RINSED
- 1 CUP FROZEN CORN KERNELS, THAWED
- 1 SMALL ONION, DICED
- 2 CLOVES GARLIC, MINCED
- 1 JALAPEÑO PEPPER, SEEDED AND DICED
- 1 TBSP OLIVE OIL
- 1 TBSP CHILI POWDER
- 1 TSP GROUND CUMIN
- SALT AND PEPPER, TO TASTE
- 1/4 CUP CHOPPED FRESH CILANTRO
- 1 LIME, CUT INTO WEDGES

INSTRUCTIONS:

1. PREHEAT OVEN TO 375°F (190°C). CUT OFF THE TOPS OF THE BELL PEPPERS AND REMOVE THE SEEDS AND MEMBRANES.
2. IN A SAUCEPAN, BRING 2 CUPS OF WATER TO A BOIL. ADD QUINOA, REDUCE HEAT TO LOW, COVER, AND SIMMER FOR 15 MINUTES OR UNTIL ALL THE WATER HAS BEEN ABSORBED. FLUFF WITH A FORK.
3. IN A SKILLET, HEAT OLIVE OIL OVER MEDIUM HEAT. ADD ONION, GARLIC, AND JALAPEÑO PEPPER AND SAUTÉ FOR 2–3 MINUTES.
4. ADD BLACK BEANS, CORN, CHILI POWDER, CUMIN, SALT, AND PEPPER. COOK FOR 5–7 MINUTES OR UNTIL THE VEGETABLES ARE TENDER.
5. ADD COOKED QUINOA TO THE SKILLET AND STIR TO COMBINE. ADD CHOPPED CILANTRO AND STIR AGAIN.
6. SPOON THE QUINOA MIXTURE INTO THE PREPARED BELL PEPPERS, PACKING IT DOWN SLIGHTLY.
7. PLACE THE STUFFED BELL PEPPERS IN A BAKING DISH AND BAKE FOR 25–30 MINUTES OR UNTIL THE PEPPERS ARE TENDER AND THE FILLING IS HEATED THROUGH.
8. SERVE HOT WITH LIME WEDGES ON THE SIDE.

THIS DISH IS NOT ONLY HEALTHY AND TASTY, BUT IT ALSO FEATURES CORN AND BLACK BEANS, WHICH ARE BOTH GREAT SOURCES OF PLANT-BASED PROTEIN AND DIETARY FIBRE. THE COMBINATION OF SPICES AND FRESH CILANTRO GIVE IT A DELICIOUS MEXICAN FLAVOUR, AND THE COLOURFUL BELL PEPPERS MAKE FOR AN IMPRESSIVE PRESENTATION. ENJOY!

GARLIC AND LEMON ROASTED BROCCOLI AND KALE SALAD WITH QUINOA AND FETA

INGREDIENTS:
- 1 LARGE BUNCH STEM BROCCOLI, CUT INTO BITE-SIZED FLORETS
- 4 CUPS KALE LEAVES, TORN INTO BITE-SIZED PIECES
- 3 CLOVES GARLIC, MINCED
- 1 LEMON, JUICED
- 2 TBSP OLIVE OIL
- 1/2 TSP SALT
- 1/4 TSP BLACK PEPPER
- 1 CUP COOKED QUINOA
- 1/2 CUP CRUMBLED FETA CHEESE
- 1/4 CUP CHOPPED FRESH PARSLEY

INSTRUCTIONS:
1. PREHEAT OVEN TO 400°F (200°C). LINE A BAKING SHEET WITH PARCHMENT PAPER.
2. IN A BOWL, TOSS BROCCOLI FLORETS WITH 1 TABLESPOON OF OLIVE OIL AND 1/4 TEASPOON OF SALT. ARRANGE THEM IN A SINGLE LAYER ON THE BAKING SHEET.
3. ROAST BROCCOLI IN THE OVEN FOR 10-12 MINUTES, UNTIL JUST TENDER AND SLIGHTLY CHARRED AROUND THE EDGES. REMOVE FROM OVEN AND LET COOL.
4. IN ANOTHER BOWL, MASSAGE KALE LEAVES WITH 1 TABLESPOON OF OLIVE OIL, LEMON JUICE, GARLIC, 1/4 TEASPOON OF SALT, AND BLACK PEPPER UNTIL LEAVES BECOME SLIGHTLY WILTED AND TENDER.
5. TO ASSEMBLE THE SALAD, COMBINE ROASTED BROCCOLI AND MASSAGED KALE IN A LARGE BOWL.
6. ADD COOKED QUINOA TO THE BOWL AND TOSS TO COMBINE.
7. SPRINKLE FETA CHEESE AND CHOPPED PARSLEY OVER THE SALAD, AND TOSS GENTLY TO COMBINE.
8. SERVE AT ROOM TEMPERATURE.

THIS DISH IS PACKED WITH NUTRIENTS FROM THE STEM BROCCOLI AND KALE, WHICH ARE BOTH RICH IN VITAMINS AND MINERALS. THE QUINOA PROVIDES ADDITIONAL PROTEIN AND FIBRE, WHILE THE FETA CHEESE ADDS A TANGY AND SALTY FLAVOUR. THE LEMON AND GARLIC DRESSING TIES EVERYTHING TOGETHER AND MAKES THIS SALAD A PERFECT BALANCE OF FLAVOURS. ENJOY!

TUNA AND WHITE BEAN SALAD WITH ARUGULA AND CHERRY TOMATOES

INGREDIENTS:

- 2 CANS TUNA IN WATER, DRAINED
- 2 CUPS COOKED WHITE BEANS, DRAINED AND RINSED
- 2 CUPS ARUGULA LEAVES
- 1 CUP CHERRY TOMATOES, HALVED
- 1/4 CUP CHOPPED RED ONION
- 2 TBSP CHOPPED FRESH PARSLEY
- 2 TBSP LEMON JUICE
- 1 TBSP DIJON MUSTARD
- 1 TBSP HONEY
- 1/4 CUP OLIVE OIL
- SALT AND PEPPER, TO TASTE

INSTRUCTIONS:
1. IN A LARGE BOWL, COMBINE TUNA, WHITE BEANS, ARUGULA, CHERRY TOMATOES, RED ONION, AND PARSLEY.
2. IN A SMALL BOWL, WHISK TOGETHER LEMON JUICE, DIJON MUSTARD, HONEY, OLIVE OIL, SALT, AND PEPPER UNTIL WELL COMBINED.
3. POUR THE DRESSING OVER THE TUNA AND WHITE BEAN MIXTURE, AND TOSS GENTLY TO COAT.
4. SERVE CHILLED OR AT ROOM TEMPERATURE.

THIS DISH IS A GREAT SOURCE OF LEAN PROTEIN AND HEALTHY FATS FROM THE TUNA AND OLIVE OIL. THE WHITE BEANS ADD ADDITIONAL PROTEIN AND FIBRE, WHILE THE ARUGULA AND CHERRY TOMATOES PROVIDE A FRESH AND VIBRANT FLAVOUR. THE DRESSING WITH A TOUCH OF HONEY GIVES THE SALAD A SWEET AND TANGY TASTE THAT COMPLEMENTS THE OTHER INGREDIENTS PERFECTLY. ENJOY!

CARROT AND PEA FRIED RICE WITH TOFU (PART 1)

INGREDIENTS:
- 2 CUPS COOKED BROWN RICE, COOLED
- 1 BLOCK OF FIRM TOFU, PRESSED AND CUT INTO SMALL CUBES
- 2 LARGE CARROTS, PEELED AND DICED
- 1 CUP FROZEN PEAS, THAWED
- 1 SMALL ONION, DICED
- 2 CLOVES GARLIC, MINCED
- 1 TBSP GINGER, GRATED
- 2 TBSP SOY SAUCE
- 1 TBSP SESAME OIL
- 1 TBSP VEGETABLE OIL
- SALT AND PEPPER, TO TASTE
- 2 GREEN ONIONS, THINLY SLICED
- 2 TBSP CHOPPED FRESH CILANTRO
- 1 LIME, CUT INTO WEDGES

INSTRUCTIONS:
1. IN A LARGE SKILLET OR WOK, HEAT VEGETABLE OIL OVER MEDIUM-HIGH HEAT. ADD CUBED TOFU AND COOK UNTIL GOLDEN BROWN AND CRISPY, STIRRING OCCASIONALLY. REMOVE FROM SKILLET AND SET ASIDE.
2. IN THE SAME SKILLET, HEAT SESAME OIL OVER MEDIUM-HIGH HEAT. ADD DICED CARROTS AND SAUTÉ FOR 2-3 MINUTES, UNTIL SLIGHTLY SOFTENED.
3. ADD ONION, GARLIC, AND GINGER TO THE SKILLET AND SAUTÉ FOR ANOTHER 2-3 MINUTES, UNTIL THE ONION IS TRANSLUCENT.

CARROT AND PEA FRIED RICE WITH TOFU (PART 2)

4.   ADD COOKED BROWN RICE, PEAS, AND SOY SAUCE TO THE SKILLET, AND STIR TO COMBINE. COOK FOR 3-4 MINUTES, UNTIL THE RICE IS HEATED THROUGH AND THE VEGETABLES ARE TENDER.

5.   ADD CRISPY TOFU TO THE SKILLET AND TOSS GENTLY TO COMBINE.

6.   SEASON WITH SALT AND PEPPER TO TASTE.

7   SERVE HOT, TOPPED WITH SLICED GREEN ONIONS, CHOPPED CILANTRO, AND LIME WEDGES ON THE SIDE.

THIS DISH IS A GREAT WAY TO INCORPORATE MORE VEGETABLES AND PLANT-BASED PROTEIN INTO YOUR DIET, WITH THE CARROTS AND PEAS PROVIDING PLENTY OF VITAMINS AND MINERALS. THE CRISPY TOFU ADDS ADDITIONAL PROTEIN AND TEXTURE, WHILE THE FRIED RICE IS FLAVOURFUL AND SATISFYING. THE FRESH CILANTRO AND LIME JUICE ADD A BRIGHT AND ZESTY FINISHING TOUCH TO THIS DISH. ENJOY!

GREEN GODDESS BUDDHA BOWL WITH ROASTED VEGETABLES AND CHICKPEAS

INGREDIENTS:
- 2 CUPS COOKED QUINOA
- 1 CAN CHICKPEAS, DRAINED AND RINSED
- 1 BUNCH KALE, STEMS REMOVED AND CHOPPED
- 1 BUNCH BROCCOLI, CUT INTO SMALL FLORETS
- 1 ZUCCHINI, SLICED INTO HALF-MOONS
- 1 AVOCADO, SLICED
- 1/4 CUP SUNFLOWER SEEDS
- 1/4 CUP TAHINI
- 1/4 CUP LEMON JUICE
- 2 CLOVES GARLIC, MINCED
- 2 TBSP OLIVE OIL
- 2 TBSP CHOPPED FRESH PARSLEY
- SALT AND PEPPER, TO TASTE

INSTRUCTIONS:
1. PREHEAT OVEN TO 400°F (200°C). LINE A BAKING SHEET WITH PARCHMENT PAPER.
2. IN A BOWL, TOSS BROCCOLI AND ZUCCHINI WITH 1 TABLESPOON OF OLIVE OIL AND 1/4 TEASPOON OF SALT. ARRANGE THEM IN A SINGLE LAYER ON THE BAKING SHEET.
3. ROAST VEGETABLES IN THE OVEN FOR 15-20 MINUTES, UNTIL TENDER AND SLIGHTLY CHARRED AROUND THE EDGES. REMOVE FROM OVEN AND LET COOL.
4. IN A LARGE BOWL, COMBINE COOKED QUINOA, CHICKPEAS, AND CHOPPED KALE.
5. TO MAKE THE DRESSING, WHISK TOGETHER TAHINI, LEMON JUICE, GARLIC, 1/4 TEASPOON OF SALT, AND BLACK PEPPER UNTIL SMOOTH. IF THE DRESSING IS TOO THICK, ADD WATER, 1 TABLESPOON AT A TIME, UNTIL DESIRED CONSISTENCY IS REACHED.
6. DRIZZLE THE DRESSING OVER THE QUINOA, CHICKPEA, AND KALE MIXTURE, AND TOSS GENTLY TO COAT.
7. DIVIDE THE MIXTURE AMONG FOUR BOWLS.
8. TOP EACH BOWL WITH ROASTED VEGETABLES, SLICED AVOCADO, SUNFLOWER SEEDS, AND CHOPPED PARSLEY.
9. SERVE AT ROOM TEMPERATURE.

THIS DISH IS PACKED WITH NUTRIENT-RICH DARK GREEN VEGETABLES SUCH AS KALE AND BROCCOLI, WHICH ARE HIGH IN VITAMINS AND MINERALS. THE CHICKPEAS AND QUINOA PROVIDE ADDITIONAL PROTEIN AND FIBRE, WHILE THE AVOCADO ADDS HEALTHY FATS. THE GREEN GODDESS DRESSING MADE WITH TAHINI AND LEMON JUICE IS RICH AND FLAVOURFUL, AND TIES EVERYTHING TOGETHER. THE ROASTED VEGETABLES ADD A SWEET AND SMOKY FLAVOUR THAT COMPLEMENTS THE OTHER INGREDIENTS PERFECTLY. ENJOY!

MIXED BERRY SPINACH SALAD WITH GRILLED CHICKEN

INGREDIENTS:
- 2 BONELESS, SKINLESS CHICKEN BREASTS
- 4 CUPS BABY SPINACH
- 1 CUP MIXED BERRIES (SUCH AS BLUEBERRIES, RASPBERRIES, AND STRAWBERRIES)
- 1/4 CUP SLICED ALMONDS
- 1/4 CUP CRUMBLED FETA CHEESE
- 1/4 CUP BALSAMIC VINEGAR
- 2 TBSP HONEY
- 2 TBSP OLIVE OIL
- SALT AND PEPPER, TO TASTE

INSTRUCTIONS:
1. PREHEAT GRILL TO MEDIUM-HIGH HEAT.
2. SEASON CHICKEN BREASTS WITH SALT AND PEPPER. GRILL FOR 5-6 MINUTES ON EACH SIDE, OR UNTIL COOKED THROUGH. LET COOL FOR A FEW MINUTES, THEN SLICE INTO STRIPS.
3. IN A LARGE BOWL, COMBINE BABY SPINACH, MIXED BERRIES, SLICED ALMONDS, AND CRUMBLED FETA CHEESE.
4. IN A SMALL BOWL, WHISK TOGETHER BALSAMIC VINEGAR, HONEY, OLIVE OIL, 1/4 TEASPOON OF SALT, AND BLACK PEPPER UNTIL WELL COMBINED.
5. DRIZZLE THE DRESSING OVER THE SALAD AND TOSS GENTLY TO COAT.
6. DIVIDE THE SALAD AMONG FOUR PLATES.
7. TOP EACH PLATE WITH SLICED GRILLED CHICKEN.
8. SERVE IMMEDIATELY.

THIS DISH IS A DELICIOUS WAY TO ENJOY THE HEALTH BENEFITS OF BERRIES, WHICH ARE HIGH IN ANTIOXIDANTS AND VITAMIN C. THE SPINACH PROVIDES ADDITIONAL VITAMINS AND MINERALS, WHILE THE CHICKEN ADDS PROTEIN. THE BALSAMIC VINAIGRETTE IS A FLAVOURFUL AND TANGY DRESSING THAT COMPLEMENTS THE SWEETNESS OF THE BERRIES. THE SLICED ALMONDS ADD A CRUNCHY TEXTURE, WHILE THE CRUMBLED FETA CHEESE ADDS A SALTY AND CREAMY ELEMENT. ENJOY!

KALE AND EEL BOWL WITH MISO DRESSING

INGREDIENTS:
- 2 FRESH EELS, CLEANED AND FILLETED
- 1 BUNCH KALE, STEMS REMOVED AND CHOPPED
- 2 CUPS COOKED BROWN RICE
- 1 AVOCADO, SLICED
- 1/4 CUP SLICED SCALLIONS
- 1 TBSP SESAME SEEDS
- 2 TBSP OLIVE OIL
- SALT AND PEPPER, TO TASTE

FOR THE MISO DRESSING:
- 1 TBSP MISO PASTE
- 2 TBSP RICE VINEGAR
- 2 TBSP SOY SAUCE
- 1 TBSP HONEY
- 1 TSP GRATED GINGER
- 1 CLOVE GARLIC, MINCED
- 2 TBSP WATER

INSTRUCTIONS:
1. PREHEAT THE OVEN TO 425°F (218°C). LINE A BAKING SHEET WITH PARCHMENT PAPER.
2. SEASON THE EEL FILLETS WITH SALT AND PEPPER. BRUSH THEM WITH OLIVE OIL AND ARRANGE THEM ON THE BAKING SHEET.
3. ROAST THE EEL FILLETS FOR 10–12 MINUTES, OR UNTIL COOKED THROUGH.
4. IN A LARGE BOWL, COMBINE THE CHOPPED KALE AND COOKED BROWN RICE.
5. TO MAKE THE MISO DRESSING, WHISK TOGETHER MISO PASTE, RICE VINEGAR, SOY SAUCE, HONEY, GRATED GINGER, MINCED GARLIC, AND WATER IN A SMALL BOWL.
6. DRIZZLE THE MISO DRESSING OVER THE KALE AND RICE MIXTURE AND TOSS GENTLY TO COAT.
7. DIVIDE THE KALE AND RICE MIXTURE AMONG FOUR BOWLS.
8. TOP EACH BOWL WITH SLICED AVOCADO, SLICED SCALLIONS, AND ROASTED EEL FILLETS.
9. SPRINKLE SESAME SEEDS ON TOP.
10. SERVE IMMEDIATELY.

THIS DISH IS A DELICIOUS WAY TO ENJOY THE UNIQUE FLAVOUR OF EEL, WHICH IS HIGH IN PROTEIN AND OMEGA-3 FATTY ACIDS. THE KALE AND BROWN RICE ADD FIBRE AND NUTRIENTS TO THE DISH, WHILE THE AVOCADO ADDS HEALTHY FATS.

TURMERIC MUSHROOM STIR-FRY

INGREDIENTS:
- 1 POUND MUSHROOMS, SLICED
- 2 CLOVES GARLIC, MINCED
- 1 ONION, DICED
- 1 TEASPOON TURMERIC POWDER
- 1 TEASPOON CUMIN POWDER
- 1/2 TEASPOON PAPRIKA
- 1 TABLESPOON OLIVE OIL
- SALT AND PEPPER, TO TASTE
- FRESH PARSLEY, CHOPPED (OPTIONAL)

INSTRUCTIONS:
1. HEAT OLIVE OIL IN A LARGE SKILLET OVER MEDIUM-HIGH HEAT. ADD SLICED MUSHROOMS AND STIR-FRY FOR ABOUT 5 MINUTES, OR UNTIL THE MUSHROOMS ARE BROWNED AND TENDER.
2. ADD DICED ONION AND MINCED GARLIC TO THE SKILLET AND STIR-FRY FOR ANOTHER 2-3 MINUTES, OR UNTIL THE ONION IS TRANSLUCENT.
3. ADD TURMERIC, CUMIN, AND PAPRIKA TO THE SKILLET AND STIR WELL TO COAT THE MUSHROOMS AND ONION EVENLY. COOK FOR AN ADDITIONAL 1-2 MINUTES, OR UNTIL THE SPICES ARE FRAGRANT.
4. SEASON WITH SALT AND PEPPER TO TASTE. GARNISH WITH FRESH CHOPPED PARSLEY, IF DESIRED.
5. SERVE HOT WITH RICE OR QUINOA FOR A HEALTHY AND DELICIOUS MEAL.

THIS TURMERIC MUSHROOM STIR-FRY IS PACKED WITH FLAVOUR AND NUTRITION. TURMERIC IS KNOWN FOR ITS ANTI-INFLAMMATORY PROPERTIES, WHILE MUSHROOMS ARE A GREAT SOURCE OF FIBRE, PROTEIN, AND VITAMINS.

WE SINCERELY HOPE THAT YOU ENJOYED THIS FUN BOOK!

IF YOU HAVE A MOMENT, A REVIEW ON AMAZON WOULD MEAN THE WORLD TO US. THANK YOU!

MORE TO COME!